# PRAISE FOR
# *GREAT MOTIVATION SECRETS OF GREAT LEADERS*

"The essence of effective leadership is persuading others to follow your lead. We call it motivation. *Great Motivation Secrets* gets to the heart of how leaders create conditions for motivation to occur by energizing their minds, encouraging their hearts, and exhorting their spirits."

—John Maxwell, America's preeminent author
on leadership and founder of Maximum Impact

"When John Baldoni writes on leadership, I pay close attention. *Great Motivation Secrets* is his best book yet. After you read it, I know you'll agree with me."

—Pat Williams, Senior Vice President, Orlando Magic

"Rousing others for common cause is essential but elusive. For fresh insight into what makes the difference, John Baldoni offers compelling portraits of leading figures who have done it, ranging from Colleen Barrett of Southwest Airlines to Magic Johnson and Ernest Shackleton. *Great Motivation Secrets of Great Leaders* reveals what we all must do if we are to be great at inspiring others to a cause."

—Michael Useem, Professor and Director of the
Wharton School's Leadership Center and author of
*Leading Up* and *The Leadership Moment*

"Leaders accomplish very little by themselves. In fact the job of leadership is to bring others along with you. That requires motivation. You can learn a great deal about how leaders motivate through example, communication, and coaching in *Great Motivation Secrets*. Baldoni reveals insights you can put into practice to achieve the right results, the right way, right now!"

—James G. O'Connor, Group Vice President,
North America Marketing Sales and Service,
Ford Motor Company

"John Baldoni has written a very readable and useful book on motivation. He mixes sound advice on motivational techniques with entertaining and relevant examples from leaders past and present to bring the subject alive. A great read."

—Personal comments of Dr. A. Peter Green,
Vice President, Pfizer Global Research & Development

"This book is a timely reminder that our success as leaders depends on our ability to successfully motivate and inspire people! John Baldoni provides us with insight into the successful motivational techniques and abilities of some of our great leaders. *Great Motivation Secrets of Great Leaders* will be required reading for everyone in our leadership development program."

—Michael L. Bivens, V.P. Kellogg's Morning Foods
Learning & Development

# GREAT MOTIVATION SECRETS OF GREAT LEADERS

## ALSO BY JOHN BALDONI

*Great Communication Secrets of Great Leaders* (2003)

*180 Ways to Walk the Motivation Talk* (coauthored with Eric Harvey) (2002)

*Personal Leadership, Taking Control of Your Work Life* (2001)

*180 Ways to Walk the Leadership Talk* (2000)

# GREAT MOTIVATION SECRETS OF GREAT LEADERS

JOHN BALDONI

**McGraw-Hill**

New York   Chicago   San Francisco   Lisbon   London   Madrid   Mexico City
Milan   New Delhi   San Juan   Seoul   Singapore   Sydney   Toronto

The **McGraw·Hill** Companies

     4  5  6  7  8  9  0    FGR/FGR    0  9

ISBN 0-07-144774-1

McGraw-Hill books are available at special quantity discounts to use as premiums and sales promotions, or for use in corporate training programs. For more information, please write to the Director of Special Sales, Professional Publishing, McGraw-Hill, Two Penn Plaza, New York, NY 10121-2298. Or contact your local bookstore.

 This book is printed on recycled, acid-free paper containing a minimum of 50% recycled, de-inked fiber.


**Library of Congress Cataloging-in-Publication Data**

Baldoni, John.
     Great motivation secrets of great leaders  /  by John Baldoni.
          p.   cm.
     ISBN 0-07-144774-1 (alk. paper)
     1.  Employee motivation.    2.  Leadership.    I. Title.

  HF5549.5.M63B355    2004
  658.3'14—dc22

                                                                    2004020173

To Gail Campanella
with love

# Contents

# Acknowledgments

The start of this book came with an e-mail from my former editor at McGraw-Hill, Barry Neville, who suggested that for my next book I consider the topic of motivation. But the origins of this book really stretch back much further, as I was reminded when I received an e-mail from another friend and author, David Cichelli. It was Dave who many years ago had introduced me to the work of Abraham Maslow for a talk I was to give. While I cannot remember anything about the talk, the connection with the ideas of Dr. Maslow stuck.

As I am a consultant focusing on leadership communication, specifically on helping men and women use their communications to achieve their goals, motivation is a natural topic for me to explore. Communication is the operative driver of the entire motivational process; it is the means by which leaders create conditions, and reinforce them, in which people can feel motivated to achieve.

My explorations have been helped by many colleagues. It was Kathy Macdonald who provided key suggestions in the development and writing stages that gave the ideas their shape and proper weight. Kevin Small of Injoy and his able colleague Colleen Johnston deserve special mention for opening doors for me. I also want to extend a special thank-you to Frances Hesselbein, who generously gave her time, and to David Hackworth, who did likewise. I also appreciate the kind introduction to Colonel Hackworth by Don Vandergriff, army officer, fellow author, and military affairs expert. Ari Weinzweig and Paul Saginaw of Zingerman's put up with my barrage of questions, and their colleague, Maggie Bayless of Zing Train, was very helpful in providing access and insight. I also want to thank Eric Harvey, with whom I cowrote an earlier book on motivation; its lessons have influenced me in this endeavor.

I also owe a big thanks to my current editor at McGraw-Hill, Donya Dickerson, for her enthusiasm in getting this project completed. The editing supervisor, Janice Race, and copy editor, Alice Manning, deserve credit for helping the manuscript read as well as it was intended to. And, of course, no book of mine would be complete without a thank-you to my wife, friend, and life partner, Gail Campanella, who helped make the entire book creation process possible and bearable.

# INTRODUCTION

*If . . . worst comes to worst,*
*I want each one of you to do his utmost to destroy our enemies.*
*If there is only one plane left to make a final run-in,*
*I want that man to go in and get a hit.*
*May God be with us all.*
*Good luck, and give 'em hell.*

*R*EADING THOSE WORDS SENDS a chill down the spine, particularly when you realize that the man who wrote them died the next morning doing exactly what he had urged his men to do. He was Lt. Comdr. Jack Waldron of Torpedo Squadron 8 of the USS Hornet. Leading his squadron of Devastator torpedo bombers, an underpowered and dangerously slow plane, right into the heart of the Japanese carrier force, Waldron and his men were mercilessly shot down by the faster and more maneuverable Zeroes and the ships' antiaircraft power. An hour and a half later, a subsequent wave of Dauntless dive bombers, led by Lt. Comdr. Wade McCluskey, struck the carrier force when it was at its most vulnerable—with some Zeroes returning from an attack low on fuel, others on the carrier deck awaiting refueling, and fuel lines looping across the deck. Within six minutes, three of the carriers were on fire and would ultimately sink. A fourth was hit later that afternoon and would also sink, but not before launching an attack on the USS Yorktown. This was the Battle of Midway, and it was won in part by what historian Victor Davis Hanson calls "pilot initiative." Inherent in this initiative was courage and bravery in the cause of something greater than themselves.[1]

Six decades later, a young competitive bicyclist was given the worst news of his young life: He had cancer, and it had spread *from his testicles to his lungs and into his brain. He was in his mid-twenties, with an ego as big as the world and a competitive urge that was perhaps as big. His name was Lance Armstrong, and he refused to give up. He ultimately beat back the cancer into remission and relaunched his bicycling career. In 1999, he won his first Tour de France title. The Tour de France is to bicycling what the Super Bowl is to pee-wee football—infinitely more competitive, grueling, and daunting. It has been called the most demanding event in all of sports. It lasts for three weeks in the middle of the French summer and covers 2,100 miles, up and down mountains, through lowlands, and along the coast. In 2004, Armstrong became the first cyclist to win six Tours; he also won them consecutively. Only four other men have ever won five Tours, and only one, Miguel Indurain, had won five consecutively. It is a testament to Armstrong's relentless training, iron will, and commitment to succeed.*

 මෙ

These two scenarios, while dramatically different in key respects, illustrate one compelling factor: that motivation, the will to go, comes from within. No one forced Waldron and McCluskey and their fellow pilots into the guns of the Japanese ships; no one forced Armstrong to race, especially after a near-death experience. It was their inner drive, their will to persevere. The pilots were fighting against a foe that had sneak-attacked them six months previously and that until that moment had seemed almost invincible. Armstrong was fighting the legacy of a disease as well as competing against scores of other cyclists. Certainly the men of Midway were heroes, and you can consider Armstrong one as well. But it is equally certain that all of them would disclaim such a title. They did what they did because it was the right thing for them to do. And that is what motivation is all about: leading oneself from within and creating those same conditions so that others can follow suit. Motivation is a genuine leadership behavior. It is essential to the leadership process because it is through the efforts of others that leaders accomplish their goals. And leaders can achieve their goals only when those goals have the support of others, when those who will be involved in achieving them want to do so.

Writing about motivation is challenging, even daunting. For one thing, a great deal has been written about it already. But the greater challenge is that some of what has been written about motivation is wrongheaded. It is rooted in a type of thinking that says that motivation can be imposed on someone. This is not correct. You can compel someone to do something, even against her will, if you use enough force or threaten her with punishment or deprivation or injuries to her loved ones. Tyrants and dictators are prime executors of coercion. But this is short-lived; it will not yield lasting or fulfilling results. Things will get done, but only halfheartedly. Motivation, by contrast, must be internalized by the individual.

It is therefore the leader's responsibility to create conditions that will enable individuals and teams to get things done in ways that they find enriching and fulfilling. If the leader does this, motivation can occur. This does not mean that leaders become namby-pamby and softhearted; it demands that they strike a balance between individuals' need for self-enrichment, literally and figuratively, and the organization's need for results. When motivation occurs, individuals become transformed; they want to achieve, they want to do well. Why? Because their work matters—to their boss, to their teams, and to themselves. The purpose of this book, then, is to demonstrate ways in which leaders can create an environment that allows people to succeed and organizations to thrive.

The leader's most powerful tool in the motivation process is communication. Communication drives the action forward, keeping leader and follower and leader and organization aligned and focused on joint goals that are meaningful and worth achieving. Communication, by nature, is a two-way process; it ensures that leader and follower understand each other, and understanding is essential to building trust. Motivation can occur only in situations in which followers trust their leaders and leaders trust their followers.

## STORY AND PRACTICE

*Great Motivation Secrets of Great Leaders* blends management principles and leadership stories. In the principles section, we will explore how managers can communicate, exemplify, coach, recognize, and sacrifice in order to create optimal conditions for motivation to occur. Each chapter will also feature a profile or two of a leader-motivator who articulates these principles through his or her personal example. While not all of the people profiled are motivators in a conventional sense, all of them motivate through their leadership actions. As a result, their stories radiate value and truth.

Among the leaders profiled in this book are the following:

- *Colleen Barrett,* a former legal secretary turned president of Southwest Airlines, the most people-friendly carrier in the air and on the ground because of its culture, which she helped create and foster

- *Colonel David Hackworth,* a highly decorated colonel whose tough actions in Vietnam transformed a group of perceived losers into a hard-core fighting team

- *Frances Hesselbein,* former CEO of the Girl Scouts of the USA and president of the Leader to Leader Institute, who has been recognized by academics and government leaders, including the president of the United States, as an accomplished leader

- *Earvin "Magic" Johnson,* a collegiate and NBA Hall of Fame basketball player who has built a very successful business by reaching out to people in the urban community, and has also established an educational foundation for disadvantaged youth.

- *Mary Kay Ash,* an entrepreneur who opened the door to financial freedom for thousands of women

- *Sam Walton,* the legendary businessman who built the largest retail chain in the world from scratch

- *Pat Summitt,* head coach of the University of Tennessee Lady Volunteers, the winningest women's basketball team in the nation and an example of how to model and develop self-directed teams

- *Thich Nhat Hanh,* a Vietnamese Buddhist author and spiritual leader who has dedicated his life to peace

- *Zingerman's,* a community of food-related businesses founded and operated by Paul Saginaw and Ari Weinzweig that has flourished by empowering people and recognizing their needs for growth and development

- *Crazy Horse,* the Sioux warrior who sacrificed his way of life and his life for the good of his people and thereby serves an example of heroism

- *Ernest Shackleton,* the legendary polar explorer, whose leadership legacy is that he did not lose a man, even though he lost his ship

These leaders are an eclectic mix. They come from different walks of life, and a few come from different periods in history. There is a unifying theme, however: Each of them knew, or knows, how to create conditions in which people can motivate themselves. Some, like Ernest Shackleton and Earvin "Magic" Johnson, are gregarious and outgoing; others, like Crazy Horse, are more soft-spoken, letting their example do the talking. Thich Nhat Hanh, Frances Hesselbein, and David Hackworth are eloquent communicators as well as outstanding manager-leaders. Pat Summitt and Colleen Barrett are coaches, one of young women, the other of an entire organization. Mary Kay Ash and Sam Walton were entrepreneurs, as are Paul Saginaw and Ari Weinzweig. Each has or had a unique style that drew people in;

people wanted to participate in whatever the leader was doing, whether it was playing a sport, running a business, or defending his or her people.

There is a perception that leaders who motivate are cheerleading, rah-rah types. Again, some are and some are not, but *all* of them lead more by example than by oratory. All of them are incredibly hardworking and committed. Leading an enterprise, whether it be a community or a business, requires tremendous effort; and that effort is particularly demanding when you have pledged to create a culture in which people matter as contributors and individuals. That effort is mentally, emotionally, and even physically taxing. It requires discipline and will.

There is no one model for how a leader must behave as a motivator, and for that reason I have included many different individuals in the hope that readers can learn from their unique approaches and find something that they can apply to their own lives or their own leadership opportunities.

In truth, there are many thousands, even millions, of effective motivators. These are the men and women who make our organizations go; their refusal to accept the status quo, coupled with a genuine affinity for people, prods them and their organizations forward. Their example, as well as their interaction with others, creates a state of raised expectations. They make people around them better. All of the leaders profiled in this book do or have done this. But I fully realize that motivation occurs every moment of every day throughout the world. It occurs when the light goes on in someone's heart or mind or spirit, and she says, "Yes, I can do that." The reason for the yes comes from within, but more often than not, it was someone close to her, either personally or through the media, who nudged her forward. That is motivation in its fullest form.

Additionally, each of these leaders has an inspirational story to tell. All of them have faced moments of truth that might have humbled a lesser individual. Each rose nobly to the occasion, and in the process became a stronger, more effective leader. And while the lessons that these leaders learned from these occasions have helped them to create the conditions in which motivation can flourish, you can apply many of these same lessons to yourself as a means of stimulating your own internal motivators.

## PRACTICAL AND PROVEN

*Great Motivation Secrets of Great Leaders* concludes with a handbook that distills key messages and leadership lessons that leaders can apply to foster a culture in which motivation can flourish for their people, their organizations, and themselves. The combination of leadership principles and stories gives this book a framework upon which managers can build as they learn how to link their individual actions to organizational results. It is my sincere hope that readers will find within these pages practical and proven techniques for bringing people together, getting them excited about the endeavor, and releasing their energies toward mutual goals.[2]

Good luck, and enjoy the process!

1

"Don't ever take a job for the money or a title. . . .
I would go for a cause anytime versus a job."

*Colleen Barrett*
*President & COO, Southwest Airlines*

# WHAT IS MOTIVATION?

*B*Y ALL RIGHTS, THEY WERE DONE IN. *Deep inside enemy territory, their putative leader dead, they should all have been slaughtered. But it didn't work out that way because their nominal leader, Cyrus the Younger, a Persian prince, was not their real leader. Their genuine leader, Xenophon, was one of their own, respected, trusted, and elected. Xenophon, a Greek general, had hired himself and his*

1

troops to help an on again–off again enemy regain his throne. In other words, Xenophon and his troops, called the Ten Thousand, were mercenaries. But however flawed their cause, their honor came to the fore in their darkest hour when they found themselves surrounded by many more thousands of enemies and thousands of miles from home.

The Greeks were superior fighters, both tactically and technologically. They knew how to fight as a team, and their swords and shields were uniquely adapted for their phalanx warfare. They also possessed the most salient edge of all: leadership. Xenophon, like all Greek commanders, led from the front; he was seen in the thick of combat, never flinching, always seeming to do the right thing. Moreover, Xenophon was more than a superior combatant; he was a shrewd strategist. He led the Ten Thousand out of Persia and across first deserts and later mountainous terrain to the safety of the sea, where they could safely embark for home. Amazingly, Xenophon returned with the majority of the Ten Thousand, incurring few casualties in war, but losing some to weather and treacherous terrain in the mountains. Historian Victor Davis Hanson attributes Xenophon's success to the superior Greek culture—not superior in a racial sense, but superior in the sense of what we today would call shared values, common purpose, and genuine leadership.[1]

Two millennia and four hundred years later, another disaster morphed into rebirth. Malden Mills in Lowell, Massachusetts, caught fire and burned to the ground. The smart business decision for the owner would have been to take the nearly $300 million in insurance money and retire; he was in his seventies, after all, and the few textile manufacturers remaining in his area were looking for any excuse to leave New England, not to stay. But not Aaron Feuerstein. Immediately after the fire, he pledged to rebuild the plant that made the popular Polartec fleece. In addition, he said that he would keep all employees on the payroll during the reconstruction. Feuerstein was hailed as a hero and received acclaim far and wide. He took this in stride, saying that he had just done the right thing. It was not the right thing finan-

*cially; the costs of meeting the payroll and reconstruction exceeded the insurance settlement.*

*A few years later, Feuerstein found himself in financial straits, and this time the employees returned the favor. They foreswore overtime and settled for lower wages in an effort to keep the plant running. It was a classic example of leadership begetting leadership. Feuerstein is a feisty sort; he does not like to share power with outsiders, and he feuded with the managers appointed by the bankruptcy court. In October 2003, Malden Mills emerged from bankruptcy. Feuerstein continued to serve in the company as chairman of the board and president in a nonexecutive role. His role model is Moses, who, according to the Bible, lived to be 120 while remaining in full possession of his faculties. By that standard, this septuagenarian has many decades more to lead the way.*[2]

ఇసా ఴు

Xenophon and Feuerstein exemplify two aspects of leadership: the personal and the organizational. Since leadership involves movement, either physical or metaphorical, other people are involved. Leaders need followers to follow them; organizations need leaders to lead them. Xenophon was the elected leader of what historians like Victor Davis Hanson call the "marching democracy." Leadership roles can and should be diffused throughout the organization so that individuals can take various of these roles without waiting for the direction or voice of a single person, but the success of the organization depends upon setting the right direction at the right time. Feuerstein demonstrated leadership in crisis, and years later his employees demonstrated their leadership by accepting lesser terms in order to keep the plant open.

Leadership comes down to two factors: trust and results. Trust encompasses the human elements of leadership: character, compassion, concern, and conviction. It is a leader's responsibility to develop trust among followers. Managers who take on a supervisory position and assume that trust will follow do so at their own peril. Employees will often do what they are supposed to do for a while at least—until the first sign of trouble. Then they will look up for guidance. If they find it, they will continue. If they don't find it, an opportunity for trust has been lost. Trust, like its complementary attribute respect, must be earned. Leaders gain trust by demonstrating that they have their people's, and, by extension, the organization's, interests at heart. That does not mean that they are pushovers; it means that they are leading with a conviction that they are doing what is best for the organization.

Emerging from the nexus of trust and results is something that all leaders need to have and in fact spend much of their time focused on. It's called motivation. Motivation is one of those topics about which much is preached with little result. The reason is simple: Leaders do not motivate—not directly, anyway. They do it *indirectly*. Motivation is an intrinsic response; it comes from inside and cannot be imposed from the outside. Motivation comes from wanting to do something of one's own free will. If you are free, you can choose to do something. Take the Greeks under Xenophon. They chose him as their general. Why? Because they believed that he had the right combination of skills and talents to lead them into battle and, as circumstances would have it, out of battle, too. The same holds for the employees at Malden Mills. While they had no say in the choice of Feuerstein as CEO, they did have a choice when it came to negotiating for a pay raise. They chose to accept lower wages because they perceived that it was in the company's best interests, as well as their own, to make a short-term sacrifice for a long-term gain.

Both the Greeks and the employees were *motivated* to do what they did. To turn the situation on its head, Xenophon could have compelled the soldiers to follow him through force—after all, that was the way things were done in the Persian army and in the army of Alexander the Great a century later—but it is doubtful that compulsion of this sort would have led so many men to safety; instead, one by one, they would have drifted away to fend for themselves. Likewise, at Malden Mills, Feuerstein could have insisted on getting a better wage deal, but he did not; the union members accepted lower wages of their own accord, thereby avoiding acrimony and building upon the loyalty Feuerstein had shown them earlier when he rebuilt the burned-out facility.

Xenophon and Feuerstein did what all successful leaders do when it comes to motivation: They created conditions in which people could motivate themselves. Since motivation comes from within, leaders need to give people reasons to believe in both themselves and the enterprise for which they work. How leaders do this is the subject of this book. There is no one way to do it, but I think it comes down to a central core of hope. Leaders need to give people a reason to believe—in themselves, the importance of what they do, and its impact on their future. All organizations that have stood the test of time, from militaries to universities, businesses to social service agencies, are built upon a foundation of followers who are motivated to serve the organization. Why? Because the organization, no matter what it does, gives them the sense that their job matters. This is their hope, and it is up to leaders to cultivate this sense of hope and to fulfill it by creating conditions in which people can motivate themselves. The question that then arises, and it is the question that all leaders ask themselves frequently, is *how*? How can *I* as the leader of my organization enable my people?

The short answer is leadership. Leadership is about getting things done the right way; to do that, you need people. To get people to follow you, you need to have them trust you. And if you want them to trust you and do things for you and the organization, they need to be motivated. Motivation is purely and simply a leadership behavior. It stems from wanting to do what is right for people as well as for the organization. If we consider leadership to be an action, motivation, too, is an active process. And if you go deep enough, motivation itself is driven by a series of actions grouped under three headings: energize, encourage, and exhort. Let's take them one at a time.

## ENERGIZE

*Energize* is what leaders do when they set the right example, communicate clearly, and challenge appropriately.

## EXEMPLIFY

Motivation starts with a good example. Leaders who hope to motivate must reflect the vision, mission, and culture of the organization they lead. What they do says more about who they are as leaders than what they say. The example they set will be the one that others follow. If the head of an organization preaches integrity and ethics in public, but in private cheats on his expense reports, then the real example he sets is one of dishonesty. By contrast, the leader who preaches the value of teamwork and volunteers to help out teams in need is demonstrating the right example. Colleen Barrett, president of Southwest Airlines, is someone who puts the needs of individuals and the organization first; she exemplifies the culture. So is Colonel David Hackworth. As a professional soldier, he put his troops' welfare ahead of his own and enabled them to succeed and survive in dangerous combat.

## COMMUNICATE

Communication is central to leadership; it includes how the leader speaks, listens, and learns. The leader who wishes to motivate must communicate a vision and a mission and follow up to check for understanding. People need to know what to do, but they also need to know that their leaders are listening. Communication encompasses more than the leader's voice; it also reflects the voice of everyone in the organization. Motivation can occur only if two-way communications occur. Thich Nhat Hanh, the Vietnamese Buddhist monk, is an eloquent writer and poet; his writings express his deep convictions as well as his calls to action on behalf of peace. Frances Hesselbein, former CEO of the Girl Scouts and now chair of the Leader to Leader Institute (formerly the Drucker Foundation), is someone who leads from the front but remains grounded in the center of her organization, focused on her mission and her commitment to diversity as she grooms leaders for the future.

## CHALLENGE

People like to be challenged. Leaders who tap into this need can achieve powerful goals because they will be linking those goals with the fulfillment of desires. The hard part of crafting a challenge is to focus on what is attainable in ways that are energizing and exciting and play upon people's imagination and creativity. Ari Weinzweig and Paul Saginaw of Zingerman's accomplished this by acknowledging the potential of their people and subsequently created a community of businesses with a vibrant culture of recognition and opportunity.

## ENCOURAGE

*Encourage* is what leaders do to support the process of motivation through empowerment, coaching, and recognition.

## EMPOWER

Leaders soon learn that their real power comes from others. It is by unleashing the individual talents and skills of other people that they can achieve their intended results. The release of this collective energy can occur only if the leader grants people the responsibility and authority to act. Empowerment is the process by which people assume responsibility and are given the authority to do their jobs. Empowerment becomes a powerful motivational tool because it puts people in control of their own destinies. However, empowerment is not an excuse to let people do what they want to do. It must encourage them to flourish within a framework of organizational goals; that is, people act on behalf of the organization and for the organization. Sam

Walton was an enterprising soul, but he built his retail organization by pushing authority to the front lines. And in the process he shared the wealth and made many employees very wealthy. Magic Johnson, too, empowers others by challenging them to take responsibility for their own lives, both personally and professionally; he has put his soul and his money into causes that improve the health and welfare of others and businesses that create new opportunities for others.

## COACH

It is a leader's responsibility to provide people with the right support to do their job. The bedrock of that support can be found in the relationship between manager and employee. The best way to nurture that relationship is through frequent and regular one-on-one coaching sessions. Coaching provides the opportunity for the leader to get to know the employee as a person and how she can help the employee achieve personal and organizational goals. Coaching also begins the process of creating the next generation of leaders. As coach of Tennessee's Lady Volunteers, Pat Summitt, by her own definition, is a combination of teacher, coach, and commander; she connects with her players on a competitive and personal level, pushing them (as well as enabling them) to succeed.

## RECOGNIZE

The need for recognition is paramount. Recognition may be the single most powerful reason that people work, aside from income. It is fundamental to our humanity that we want people to recognize what we do and how we do it. When people are recognized, they become motivated; they want to do the work, and they want to do it well. Leaders who recognize their people demonstrate their appreciation for how work is done. They also begin to build the foundation for a culture of recognition. Few people ever put more into recognition than Mary Kay Ash. She built a business upon the principle of sharing praise along with sharing the rewards.

## EXHORT

*Exhorting* is how leaders create an experience based upon sacrifice and inspiration that prepares the ground upon which motivation can flourish.

## SACRIFICE

The truest measure of service is sacrifice, putting the needs of others ahead of your own. When employees see their leaders put other people first and do it by putting aside their own ambitions, they learn to trust their leaders. Sacrifice is a form of commitment to others. It is a measure of leadership because in sacrifice we discover character and conviction, which are both essential to create the conditions in which motivation can occur. Crazy Horse, as a warrior leader, put the needs of his tribe first, even when it meant danger to himself and his way of life.

## INSPIRE

Motivation really comes down to inspiration. Since motivation comes from within, it is a form of self-inspiration. This process is nurtured by watching others achieve their goals. Most often it is developed by following the example of leaders who do the right thing for people, communicate frequently, empower vigorously, coach regularly, and sacrifice for others. Ernest Shackleton did not rescue his men from the Antarctic himself; he created conditions in which his men could believe in themselves and in each other, and by doing so he inspired them to reach beyond themselves. And in the process, survive!

All of these actions, individually and collectively, work to create a climate in which motivation can occur in individuals, teams, and the entire organization. The more a leader incorporates these actions into his leadership outlook, the better motivator he will become and the more motivated the organization will be. Each of these steps naturally facilitates motivation, and for this reason I devote a chapter to each one.

## THE FACTS ON MOTIVATION

The need for motivation is very real. In his book *The Rise of the Creative Class*, Richard Florida describes those who use their knowledge to create something new and different as members of the "creative class," a group that includes some 38 million people. According to Florida, creatives are those who earn a living by "creating meaningful new forms"; these include designers, engineers, and learned professionals in health care, law, and financial services.[3] Using survey data gathered in 2001 by *Information Week*, a leading IT publication, Florida identified a number of factors that influence motivation at work for IT professionals, whom he identifies as members of the creative class. Money was a factor, but it ranked fourth, behind challenge, flexibility, and stability. Of the respondents, 67 percent said that they wanted "challenge and responsibility" in the workplace, 53 percent sought flexibility, 43.5 percent wanted stability, and 38.5 percent said that base pay was important. Other key factors noted by more than 20 percent of the respondents were job atmosphere, casual attire, training, contribution to success, and recognition.[4]

While Florida's research pertains to IT professionals, and by extension to other creatives, the lessons from it pertain to anyone who manages bright, knowledgeable, and talented employees. You need to develop a work environment that offers challenges, grants responsibility, and offers a degree of flexibility as well as an opportunity for growth and development and recognition. All of these factors are in addition to pay. When these factors are not present, workers become dissatisfied, and their interest and subsequent productivity decline. They also will look for opportunities to leave, thereby wasting the organization's investment in their training and development.

An influential survey by *McKinsey Quarterly*, conducted in 1997, at the height of the dot.com boom, identified four key segments of workers: those who wanted to "go with a winner"; those who liked "big risk, big reward"; those who wanted to "save the world"; and those who preferred a balanced, flexible "lifestyle."[5] A follow-up study done in 2001, in the midst of a recession, not only confirmed the previous study's findings but asserted that finding talented employees was harder than ever. Of the managers surveyed, 89 percent said that it was more difficult to hire talented people, and 90 percent said that it was more difficult to retain them.[6]

Another survey, by Towers Perrin, a leading human resources consulting firm, provided additional impetus for the notion that employees want greater flexibility as well as more development. In this survey, 42 percent wanted "work-life balance," and 28 percent said that they wanted to develop their skills.[7]

These statistics illustrate that talented, creative people, the ones that every employer wants, have demands that must be met. If those demands are not met, they will leave. In October 2003, just as the nation was emerging from the recession, the Society of Human Resources published a survey stating that eight in ten workers wanted to leave their jobs.[8] There is another element lurking beneath these facts; it is fear. Recent Gallup research also shows that a prevalent factor in the workplace is fear.[9] So, if you are a manager, you must realize that many of your employees are at least considering leaving, and if they are not leaving they are fearful.

According to Bob Nelson, one of the world's foremost authorities on motivation and the author of several best-selling books on the topic, motivation is not only good for morale; it's good for business. Nelson cites a few examples. Pizza Hut asked employees for ways to reduce paperwork; the response led the company to shed a "few layers of management" as well as increase sales by 40 percent. Goodyear Tire & Rubber utilizes open-book management when it comes to departmental and plant productivity. As a result, shifts can track their own productivity and display the results for all to see. And Enterprise-Rent-A-Car posts the "financial results of every branch office" where employees can see them. Such publicity sparks "friendly rivalries" between branches. Managers, too, get caught up in the fun; the winning branch is treated to a victory party thrown by the other branches.[10] Motivation is not only good for the soul; it's good for business.

Has there ever been a greater need for managers to create a desirable, hospitable, productive work environment in which employees can find challenges and be rewarded financially, emotionally, and psychically? Perhaps, but this research is only the tip of the iceberg. You have only to talk to the employees of your own organization as well as colleagues and friends in other organizations to understand the enormousness of the challenges ahead. Managers can have a positive impact and make a positive difference if they focus their time and energy on creating conditions in which motivation can occur. The good news is that this investment will pay off in ways that benefit the organization, the employee, and the manager. Motivation is not something that's nice to do. It's a must-do, but it's a must-do that pays dividends for all who participate.

## NOTE ON FEAR

Many times managers are under the impression that they need to be tough in order to motivate. They often choose to be hard on their people, instilling a sense of fear in them in order to keep them focused on the task. And, true enough, using fear as a weapon may be an effective way to get things done. New workplace studies are showing that bosses who are bullies are effective in achieving results. In fact, many of these bosses get results that make them look good. And, sadly, employees go along with them, with good workers even covering for less productive workers. Still, bully bosses are no treat to work with, and their abusive behavior rubs off on underlings, who adopt it as part of their own work habits. Fortunately, the converse is also true: Bosses who are compassionate and concerned are emulated, too. When bosses rule by fear, workers cling together as a means of coping;

those who do not coalesce are more vulnerable to intimidation. Ironically, it is these individuals who are likely to speak up in an attempt to save their jobs.[11]

It is true that fear can be a form of management; a touch of fear may push someone to do better for a short time, but only for a short time. You can compel people to do their job by screaming and yelling at them, berating them, or even threatening to fire them. Fear or, better, compulsion works. But it works on only a single level. You engage the body, but not the heart or the mind. In other words, you gain compliance but not commitment. Worse, you fail to create a relationship; you fail to engage the whole person. Whatever the job, mental or physical, it requires the mind and sometimes the heart. Look at it from the employee's viewpoint. If the employee despises her boss, she will do little to pitch in with ideas. Nor should she. The boss becomes isolated, surrounded by the levers of power but without any *real* power. Sure he can hire and fire, but for what end? Compelling through fear is a short-term game.

One of the saddest things about compulsion is that it perpetuates itself. Those who rule *by* fear are those who have been ruled *in* fear. Like serial wife beaters, they think that all issues can be solved by the raised voice or the cocked fist. If this logic held true, then the Soviet Union would have become and would have remained the most powerful nation on earth. It was a society whose bosses ruled by compulsion, intimidation, and violence. Fear was an operative principle from top to bottom of the regime. As a result, creativity and innovation were nearly nonexistent save for some ivory-tower places.

While bosses who bully may make their numbers, they inflict considerable psychic damage on their employees. As a result, these bosses never earn the respect or the trust of their people. Both are essential to genuine leadership, and while bosses who bully may not care about leadership, or may have the sadly mistaken idea that abusive behavior is leadership, in time their behavior will catch up to them in two ways. First, abusive bosses are control freaks; they tell everyone what to do without seeking ideas or advice from their people, and as a result, they assume all authority without delegating decision making. Also, which may be surprising to some, many abusive bosses live in a state of fear themselves; they are afraid that someone above them will ask for something they cannot deliver. Such bosses live with the weight of the department on their shoulders, and eventually they will sink under its load. And second, abusive bosses can never count on their people in tough times. Abused employees will flee at the first sign that the ship is sinking. Or, better yet, they will jump to another ship where the crew is better treated, leaving the abuser boss to bail himself out.

The bottom line is, ruling by fear is self-defeating. The boss must do all the thinking; he must dictate what must be done without soliciting input or ideas from his subordinates. All ideas come from above and must be obeyed, even when they are pitifully flawed and known to be so. Management by fear is enervating; it saps the energy of the boss, and it drains the energy of the employees. No one has time to think; everyone goes through the motions like robots. And when the compliance is never challenged, it can lead to obsolescence or oblivion. Just like the Soviet Union. Managing by fear is a dead-end game that can be rectified only when managers, prodded by their employees, come to realize that it is better to provide hope and inspiration than coercion and compulsion.

Fear is not the only demotivating factor in the workplace. Just as leaders can create conditions in which people can motivate themselves, they can also create conditions in which people *demotivate* themselves. Ruling by fear is a deliberate act, but many other demotivators arise from lack of attention. For example, managers may not take the time to communicate or to coach. Managers may feel that challenging their employees is not their business, and they certainly do not want to share any power, so empowerment is a no-no. Recognition is ignored. Sacrifices do occur, but it is the organization that suffers. When employees are apathetic, what do they do? They reduce their productivity or fail to contribute more than the minimum. Why? Because they do not care. But their failure to care stems directly from the fact that they do not have a sense of ownership in the enterprise. They feel distinctly unmotivated, and this is a direct result of a management that failed to engage its people and as a result ignored their potential. Not only is this a loss in productivity, it is a loss in trust and a failure of leadership.

## ACT OF PERSUASION

Leadership is an act of persuasion to a point of view that embraces doing good for individuals, teams, and the organization. That's the ideal. The reality is that leadership is persuasion to a point of view that is good for the organization but involves tough choices about teams and individuals. It is up to the leader to make the right call at the right time. Often the choices are difficult and painful. For presidents, it might mean going to war for self-preservation or negotiating for peace at the risk of terror. For CEOs, it may be closing a plant that employs thousands or keeping the plant open and risking fiscal uncertainty. For managers, it may involve promoting one highly talented individual over another highly talented individual. All of these decisions, whether macro or micro, occur frequently. It is up to the leader to prepare to meet these challenges by understanding the nature of what leaders deliver.

## RAISING EXPECTATIONS

Motivation, as we have stated, is intrinsic. Therefore, the secret to creating motivation from within is to raise expectations, those of the group and those of the individual. By raising expectations, you challenge the status quo, but, by extension, you also give people the opportunity to participate. As we shall see, all of the leaders profiled in this book motivated by raising expectations as well as by providing a means to fulfill them. Whether it was a matter of survival or a matter of pushing the organization to a new level, or even a matter of winning a game, expectations and their potential for fulfillment played a critical role in the leader's ability to connect with his or her people on a personal level. Another way to look at expectation is as engagement. All leaders engage the minds of their people; they connect in ways that make sense. Inspired leaders engage the hearts of their people; they connect on a deeply personal level. This level is personal because individuals internalize the leader's message and make it their own. They do what the leader expects because they want to. That is the secret of motivation: getting people to do something because they want to. But this can occur only if the leader puts his values, convictions, and beliefs into practice in ways that set a good example and inspire people to follow.

## Insights into Motivation: Abraham Maslow

Abraham Maslow, a behavioral psychologist and theorist, developed a hierarchy of needs. Maslow envisioned this hierarchy as a pyramid with five levels. Starting at the base, the five levels, in ascending order, are physiological, safety, social, esteem, and self-actualization needs. The first three are important to health and well-being; that is, we need food and shelter, protection from the elements and from enemies, and a community of other people. Each must be satisfied before you can move to the next level. Esteem, the fourth level, is intrinsic—a need for recognition to validate our self-worth. Self-actualization, the highest level, is something that all of us strive to achieve—fulfillment in doing what we want to do. Motivation plays an integral role throughout the hierarchy because it propels us to do what we do to take care of ourselves and find enrichment.[12]

## Motivation Planner

"Motivation" according to General Dwight D. Eisenhower, "is the art of getting people to do what you want them to do because they want to do it." Use the following questions to assess your situation and how you might begin to create conditions in which people would feel more motivated.

Think about where you work and the people who work there. As you think, consider the following:

1. Why do people come to work? For a paycheck? For recognition?
2. Do people feel motivated, i.e., do they like to be at work because it is an enriching experience? If not, what is missing?
3. Consider the motivation model, then think about the people in your organization.
   - Are the leaders setting the right example?
   - Are the leaders communicating?
   - Are the leaders challenging their people?
   - Are the leaders empowering others?
   - Are the leaders coaching?
   - Are the leaders recognizing?
   - Are the leaders sacrificing?
   - Are the leaders inspiring?
4. What could you do to improve the climate for motivation?

## COLLEEN BARRETT

It might strike you as odd that a company known for its love of its customers and its employees (not to mention a downright sense of wackiness) was born in an environment of conflict. "The warrior mentality, the very fight to survive, is what created our culture."[13] She would know; she's Colleen Barrett, president and COO of Southwest Airlines. When Herb Kelleher, the chairman, co-founded the airline, she was his legal secretary. Today she is president and chief operating officer.

Barrett is everyone's favorite grandmother, and, in fact, she really is a grandmother. She attends many corporate parties, writes cards to employees, and watches over the human side of the company as if it were her own family. Herb Kelleher says, "She nurtured and she produced a culture which is truly extraordinary, where people feel cared for. They feel wanted. They feel they can be individualistic. They don't have to wear masks to work."[14]

## ENJOY WORK

So which is it—war or love? Both really. Southwest Airlines was a start-up airline at a time when start-up airlines were not welcomed with open arms (as if there really were ever a time when they were). Kelleher, a corporate lawyer, drew up the plan for the airline with a partner, Rollin King. The year was 1966, and their plan was a Texas-only air service. It took five years of legal brawling to get the airline into the air on June 18, 1971. But that was not the end of the fight. The major carriers wanted Southwest booted from Love Field in Dallas, which would have bankrupted the upstart airline. After more legal battles, Southwest finally won. Since 1973, when the airline first made a profit, it has not looked back; every year, through recessions, wars, and the September 11 tragedy that put many airlines into a coma, Southwest has prevailed.[15] But how? Ask Barrett or Kelleher, or any of the employees of the company, and the answer you will get is this: the people and their culture.

Barrett puts it this way. "We want people to have fun at work. We don't want them to think that work is, you know, this professional stuffy, stereotype, you know, leave your personality at home and become this robotic Stepford wife–type deliverer

[of] whatever it is that you do."[16] Recognition is essential at Southwest. Barrett understands how important it is to acknowledge a job well done; she writes personal notes and makes personal appearances at employee gatherings. As Kevin and Jackie Freiberg put it in *Nuts!*, their in-depth and passionately personal look at the company, "Celebrating people for their accomplishments is not just Southwest's way of saying 'thank you,' it is also a way the company raises the level of motivation within the company."[17]

The outward signs of Southwest's culture are visible in corporate headquarters. The corridor walls are adorned with ten thousand–plus whimsical photographs: of pets, Herb as Elvis or in drag, miniskirted flight attendants, and "Southwest planes gnawing on competitors' aircraft." Other icons of Southwest's culture are "teddy bears, pickled hot peppers, and pink flamingoes."[18] And then there are the parties, from weekly happy hours on Southwest's rooftop during good weather to annual Halloween costume parties. This does not count the many other parties marking birthdays, anniversaries, and other special events.

To Colleen Barrett, this environment is "comfortable." Referring to the pictures on the walls, she says, "This is an open scrapbook. We aren't uptight. We celebrate everything. It's like a fraternity, a sorority, a reunion. We are having a party!" Southwest isn't the only one celebrating. The man who has the contract for picture frames now has a business, according to Barrett, with 13 employees. That is a lot of celebrating. Or, put another way, a lot of recognition for a lot of people.[19]

## KEEPING THE FLAME BURNING

Successful cultures do not just happen; they are nurtured. Even today Southwest takes the job seriously. Since the mid-1990s, Southwest has initiated "culture programs" in all the cities in which it operates; "ambassadors" serve as point people to "disseminate corporate news" as well as "foster team spirit." Burnout is an issue; in 1997 the company established a "second wind team of 20 employees" whose job it was to help alleviate stress; they do this by creating libraries of self-help books as well as giving "90-minute seminars on burnout."[20]

Occasionally cracks appear. In 2003, labor unions picketed. Calls for "big airline pay" echoed throughout the company.[21] In typical Southwest fashion, the unions were not perceived as hostile. "We want a contract as soon as possible because we believe our flight attendants deserve a pay increase," said Ginger Hardage, corporate communications vice president.[22] And in 2004, rising costs of aviation fuel caused the airline to offer buyout packages to its employees. Still, as Barrett notes, "If money were the only motivator, probably half of our directors and officers wouldn't be here, because most of them could go out and earn more money elsewhere."[23]

## BUSINESS SUCCESS

Make no mistake, Southwest Airlines means business. In 2003, it carried an average of 5.5 million passengers per month, adding up to some $6 billion in revenue and $442 million in profit. From 1972 to 2002, its stock value has grown at an annualized rate of 26 percent. Its market cap is in excess of $11.7 billion. This performance has earned Southwest top 10 ranking in *Fortune* magazine's Most Admired Companies for six years running.[24]

Southwest, however, is so confident of its culture that it allowed itself to be the host of a reality television show, *Airline*. The program delivered an "unfiltered look at the workaday lives of Southwest staffers and their customers." Although it was panned by the *New York Times*, the program was popular with Southwest employees; in fact, the company threw parties when the program premiered in January 2004.[25]

## HARD WORK

Despite the fun-and-games atmosphere that is so prevalent at Southwest, people are expected to work very hard. "Part of our working environment means working our butts off," says Barrett.[26] Hard work is part of the culture. As Kevin and Jackie Freiberg point out, sacrifice is part of the culture. They note that

Barrett and Kelleher typically work "sixteen hour days . . . seven days a week."[27] Some of that sense of sacrifice comes from what the Freibergs refer to as the leadership team's commitment to servant leadership. Servant leaders, a philosophy first articulated by Robert Greenleaf in his book *Servant Leadership*, are those who put the needs of the organization first and do what they can to "serve" those needs. As the Freibergs wisely note, people feel an affinity to such leaders. The people of Southwest are no different; this is part and parcel of why they work for the airline.[28]

Another reason is a sense of ownership. Since the early 1970s, employees have owned a stake in the airline, which is publicly traded. Gary Barron, one-time senior executive at Southwest, says, "Our people think like owners and have for some time."[29] Again, the Freibergs point out that when you own something, you tend to take particular care of everything about it. As an owner, you are willing to make sacrifices for the good of the business.[30] Southwest's employees, while unionized, work with greater degrees of flexibility; pilots pick up trash in the airplane, and ticket agents may pitch in with baggage handling.[31]

Ownership also stipulates that everyone do their fair share. Young employees who join Southwest may be lulled by the culture into thinking that every day is a holiday. That's where the other side of the culture—the warrior ethic—shows. Barrett says, "Peer pressure is very intense." Those who do not hew the line are let go. Says Barrett, "We won't let it drag on."[32] Tough love also rules. In *Nuts!*, Barrett explained her point of view about Southwest being a "family": "We've had to remove people from positions around here whom I consider close personal friends and it broke my heart. But, by their own admission, it was the best thing for them and clearly the best thing for the company." Barrett, like Kelleher, believes that honesty with employees is essential. Keeping unproductive employees, or those who do not embrace Southwest's values, on board hurts the organization as well as the individual.[33]

On the flip side, Southwest Airlines looks to stretch people's capabilities as a means of motivating them. "Most organizations think you have to have an expertise in something before you can be a leader," says Barrett, who takes a more flexible approach. Kelleher credits Barrett with "put[ting] people where they can have a positive impact and grow."[34] Mistakes will occur, but Southwest understands that this is part of the process. It also encourages people to challenge authority and to ask questions. Many start-up enterprises grow up with this attitude, but forget it as maturity sets in. Not Southwest! As a vibrant marketing machine, it loves to do things new and differently. One idea did not click—same-day delivery. Still, the person who initiated it was not fired; he was forgiven. It is all part of the long-term development process.[35]

## CULTURE RULES

The strength of the culture helped the company survive a situation that many start-ups do not—replacing the founder. The job of replacing a legend at the helm is never easy. Southwest not only survived, it kept its sense of whimsy. Prior to stepping down as CEO, Herb Kelleher quoted Jim Parker, his eventual successor as CEO, as saying, "Well, Colleen's going to handle the smoking, and I'm going to handle the drinking."[36] Kelleher moved to chairman, Parker to vice chairman and CEO, and Barrett to president and COO. The company, and the culture, did not miss a beat. In July 2004, Gary Kelly became CEO upon the unexpected retirement of Jim Parker. Again, the culture survived.

"Our first customer is our employees," acknowledges Barrett. "Second is our passengers and third are our stockholders. If employees are happy, then the passengers are happy. If the passengers are happy, they come back and that makes our stockholders happy."[37] This virtuous cycle renews the culture. It assures employees that they are doing the right job. Barrett notes that after September 11, many employees felt that they were not helping their customers enough.

Our employees have become more empathetic with the customer in the sense of what an airport experience is like because of all the changes in security and changes in just the look and feel of an airport. I think it's a pretty exciting thing when one of your biggest complaints from your employees is that they aren't able to provide as good a customer-service attention as they'd like to provide because they are limited in their exchanges.[38]

And so a company with a culture forged in war has emerged as the envy of the airline industry, not to mention other industries, too, because it is an organization that puts people first. The individual most responsible for that mindset, and for nurturing the culture along the way, is Colleen Barrett. Perhaps you can sum up Barrett's attitude toward her employees this way: "If you work hard and if you treat people with respect, [they] will never disappoint you in life."[39] Lessons for any motivator to take to heart!

---

## Leadership Lessons in Motivation

- *Create a strong culture.* Southwest Airlines' employees are committed to what they do and how they do it. The way people feel about themselves and their colleagues owes a great deal to the culture that Colleen Barrett has helped to foster.

- *Be visible.* Colleen Barrett is everywhere within Southwest Airlines. She attends parties and corporate gatherings and makes herself seen and heard.

- *Show strength.* The airline industry is not for the faint of heart. You have to be strong and make tough decisions. Colleen Barrett is and does.

- *Allow people to lead.* People at Southwest are not put into boxes. Colleen Barrett sees to it that they have opportunities to grow and to develop their talents and skills.

- *Treat people right.* Colleen Barrett hits the nail on the head when she speaks of treating people well; it is common sense that she has parlayed into a successful business with hundreds of thousands of motivated employees.
- *"Walk the talk."* Colleen Barrett does what she says she will do and expects the same of everyone else. Values are fundamental to Southwest Airlines, and she makes certain that everyone understands and practices them.

# Energize

- *Exemplify*
- *Communicate*
- *Challenge*

**M**otivation requires energy. More particularly it requires the release of energy directed toward meaningful goals. Leaders have the obligation to energize their people by setting the right example and communicating what people need to do. Going one step further, it is up to leaders to challenge their people, giving them the push they need to get started.

"My job was soldier simple: It began with leading from up front. I just followed Rule Six of the old Army's Principles of Leadership: Know your soldiers and look out for their welfare."

*Colonel David H. Hackworth*
*U.S. Army, retired*

# EXEMPLIFY

## THE GIVING LIFE

*F*OR ANYONE WHO HAS EVER WONDERED, *while watching a documentary about disadvantaged people, if one person can make a difference, Susie Krabacher can answer yes! The documentary she watched was about children in Mongolia; a friend persuaded her that there were problems in her own hemisphere. Krabacher spends about three weeks of every eight work-*

ing with the poor in Haiti, the poorest country in the Western Hemisphere. Since 1994, she has established a food kitchen, a children's hospital, health-care facilities, and a string of six schools. She has also built an orphanage for "disabled and terminally ill children" as well as an orphanage for "normal children."[1]

Ms. Krabacher did not aspire to a career in community service. Once upon a time, she was a Playmate (Miss May 1983), lived in the Playboy Mansion, and dated rock stars. Later she moved to Aspen, where she still resides with her husband, an attorney. She was also a local businesswoman, owning a share of a boutique and a sushi bar. Her first stop was Cité Soleil, one of Haiti's most notorious slums. The people were wary of her at first; some hurled stones. "I called out to them not to hurt me, that I wanted to help, but because they speak Creole, no one understood," she recalls. "It took about three years before I was really accepted by the people, as they learned and believed in what I was trying to do."[2] But her life changed on her first visit to Haiti. "It changed my life. It rocked my world. I knew why I had been born that day," says Krabacher. She sold her businesses and put the money toward the people of Haiti.[3]

Her health has suffered; she has sought treatment for encephalitis, scabies, lice, and mange. Her safety, too, has been imperiled by voodoo priests and bureaucratic bribe seekers.[4] She has not given up. "She literally takes the kids nobody else wants, the throwaway children left for dead," says Tracy Chapman, a board member of her foundation, Worldwide Mercy and Sharing. Personal involvement is her calling. When local doctors and nurses wouldn't treat the sick children, she got assistance from friends in Aspen, one of whom gave her a "homegrown recipe for treating dehydration, a major killer." Krabacher says, "I never felt repulsed by any of the kids, whether they were really sick in the hospital or we found them abandoned on a piece of tin or cardboard."[5]

Tall, tanned, and beautiful, Krabacher, nicknamed "Mame Blanche" by the locals, leverages her influence in Washington *and in corporate America. She lobbies Congress for aid and flies free to Haiti on American Airlines, which has flown food to the island in support of her efforts. Each year she raises in excess of $200,000 for her foundation. As she told the* Wall Street Journal, *displaying a strong sense of humor in reference to her husband's support, "Neither of us wanted kids. Now we have 2,000 and no stretch marks to show for it."*[6] *No stretch marks perhaps, but certainly a stretched heart that embraces the children of Haiti who cannot do without her.*

There is an adage that says that the mark of character is what you do when no one is watching. Susie Krabacher would have no problem if all the lights went out. The same cannot be said about the robber barons of the late 1990s and early 2000s. In fact, the parties they threw, their palatial vacation homes, the pension plans they lavished on themselves and their favorites were out in the open. What was sorely lacking in this pseudo-potentate lifestyle was accountability to shareholders. They used equity in public companies the way Imelda Marcos bought shoes; nothing was too good for them. Their actions, even if not always found to be criminal by the courts, demonstrated one salient feature: These were not managers who set a good example.

It is therefore not surprising that few of those left behind in the companies these people fleeced have much good to say about their deposed leaders. They scorn their actions and feel shamed by them. Worse, they feel duped. After all, these were supposed to be corporate leaders to whom they entrusted their careers and their pensions. As a result, there was a sense of collective deflation. Curiously, when new management, some appointed by the courts or shareholder groups, came in, they found that there was something of value to be saved. Those employees still remaining in the legacy organizations now have something to be proud of. The new management did not win friends overnight, but over time, these managers have done what all good managers do: take care of the details and begin to manage with integrity and honesty. In other words, they lead by example.

## POWERFUL MESSAGE

Example is perhaps the most powerful leadership action. What Krabacher does to help the children of Haiti is to live the life of good example. On the corporate side, when employees hear their managers asking their people to forgo pay raises to help the company in bad times, yet see those same managers lining their own pockets with pension benefits that are not available to all employees, it leaves a bad taste. When a leader says one thing and does another, employees immediately sense it. For example, a corporate leader who espouses family values but cheats on his wife may not send the company into ruin, but he does fray the bonds of trust. I am not referring to marriages gone bad; divorce is a reality that tears apart many good men and women. What I am referring to is serial philandering; duplicity in the home leads to duplicity at work.

Let's take another, smaller issue. When managers discuss the challenges ahead and ask their people to put in extra hours, yet themselves manage to vanish at the sight of real work, it sets a bad example. Ari Weinzweig of Zingerman's, a multimillion-dollar community of food businesses, makes it a practice to wait on tables in his restaurant. He was even seen cleaning up in the wake of a children's party where some of the children ate a little too many sweet things and promptly regurgitated them onto the floor. Weinzweig could have called one of his hourly staffers to clean up the mess for him, but no. He mopped it up himself, thereby impressing the parents of the kids, and also sending a powerful message to employees that we're all in this enterprise together. Entrepreneurs understand example better than anyone because when they were getting started, they did it all. Managers in large organizations feel disassociated from customers and other levels of managers, so they tend to look away. The concept of leading by example somehow seems less tangible. This is unfortunate, since the employees of large organizations often need to be shown the right way more than employees in other businesses. Why? Because you can make yourself small (and thereby disappear) in large organizations, whereas there are not so many places to hide in smaller companies.

## THE RIGHT EXAMPLE

Leadership is about setting the right example. When people see the leader doing the right thing, they will be motivated to follow that example without being told. Proper example is the foundation of a strong culture. Good example emerges from being honest and acting in accordance with convictions. People want their leaders to be ethical, honest, and real. When leaders are real, people will be motivated to follow their example. Colonel David Hackworth, like most good commanders, always led from the front. He trained alongside his men and coached them on the big issues as well as the small. He was there for them, amid the blood, the sweat, and the muck.

The question arises, then: From where does good example emerge? It is set by leaders, men and women managers who embody the mission, vision, and values of the organization. It is true that the managers of corrupt organizations, like crime syndicates, also embody organizational values, but those values tend to be disharmony, disrespect, and dishonesty. It's better to focus on the higher moral ground, or organizations in which people try to do the right things. Colleen Barrett is someone who sets the right example. Her presence is palpable throughout the airline, but it only begins with her because the culture she has fostered has been spread by others. So how can leaders foster good example? Let's cite some ways.

- *Lead from within.* You must learn to lead yourself before you can lead others. The concept of personal leadership is a powerful one. It demands three things: autonomy (willingness to be in charge), initiative (willingness to make a positive difference), and responsibility (willingness to be accountable).[7] Personal leaders are those who have both a strong sense of self and a strong moral character. Consider President Jimmy Carter. More than two decades after leaving the White House, he won the Nobel Peace Prize because of his relentless commitment to using negotiations to end bloodshed and aid in the eradication of disease. Carter is a spiritual man, and he walks in a sense of spirit as he leads others.

- *Demonstrate conviction.* A leader needs to stand for something besides herself. Those leaders who effect change are those who were forged with a strong set of values and embody those values in their daily lives when they make the tough decisions. Congressman John Lewis of Georgia was a young man at the time of the civil rights movement in the late fifties and sixties. Tongue-tied as a youngster, he worked hard to overcome his speech impediment, and as a result became an eloquent spokesman for civil rights. He also put his body and his life on the line many times, risking beatings and repeated jailings. His young adulthood was forged by the white heat of oppression, but he emerged as a strong voice for righteousness.

- *Do what you say you will do.* Sounds simple, right? The biggest lesson that managers fail to learn is the need to live up to their promises. Sometimes this is because circumstances have changed and they can avoid the commitment. This is wrongheaded. If you commit to something, do it. If you say you will provide resources for a team, but you fail to deliver, then you must explain yourself. The reason so many people distrust politicians is that they say one thing in order to get elected, but do another in order to stay elected. Politicians on all sides do this. When you make a commitment, live by it. For example, when John McCain was running for the presidency in 2000 against George W.

Bush, he championed campaign finance reform. It was an issue that burned him once when he took campaign finance money from a banker who proved to be fraudulent. McCain repaid the money, and in the process dedicated himself to eradicating the soft money that greases the wheels of government. Even though he lost the election, he followed through on his commitment and with Senator Russ Feingold passed a campaign finance reform bill.

- *Show compassion.* Leadership involves people, and people have a multiplicity of needs, physical, emotional, and spiritual. A compassionate leader understands the complexity of the human psyche as well as the forces acting upon us from work, family, and community. Good leaders look to provide a better place for their people, be it at work, at home, or both. Bob Stoops, the head football coach at Oklahoma, insists that his coaches observe family night during the football season. Coaches are notorious for putting in hours that would make a workaholic blush. Stoops, who has won two national championships, reports for work at 8:45 a.m. after taking his children to school. He also insists on schedules that enable his coaches to balance work and life, too.

- *Live the culture.* Leaders are creatures of their environment, but unlike most creatures, they are also movers of it. As movers of and within the organization, they push it forward, at the same time shaping it as much as it shapes them. Leaders of vibrant and robust organizations must embody those organizations' values. A good example of this is the U.S. Coast Guard. Its mission is both service and protection. It serves the maritime community, both recreational and professional, with navigational and rescue assistance. It also protects our waterways from criminal and terrorist forces. Its leadership understands that the organization walks a thin line between an armed force and a rescue operation. This is a delicate balancing act, but the Coast Guard performs it well.

At the same time, if a culture has soured and is working against the very people in it, then the leader must change it. Remember the biblical story of Moses coming down from the mountaintop. After receiving the Ten Commandments the first time, he found the Israelites engaged in pagan rituals. Moses hurled the tablets in rage and stormed back up the mountain. His anger so shamed his people that they soon fell back into line. Moses had reshaped the culture.

## EXAMPLE FIRST

When leaders put these five elements into practice, they will be leading by example. And when you lead by example, you enable others to follow you. Why? Because they will want to. Their wanting to follow is essential to their motivation; they are following because they perceive that you are doing the right thing. Your example becomes their example. Historian and author James McGregor Burns wrote in his seminal study *Leadership* that people follow a leader because they want to emulate the leader's values. In the case of fatally flawed organizations like the Nazi Party or the Ku Klux Klan, emulation can be a bad thing; it leads to racial hatred and oppression. Emulation within a good or benign organization becomes a sharing process that embraces goals and objectives that will contribute to good things for people, the organization, and its stakeholders.

Motivation, therefore, must be rooted in example. Otherwise it will ring hollow. People will hear what a leader says, but unless they see her do what she says she will do, they will not be interested in following her. By contrast, when they see a leader genuinely leading by good example, they will feel motivated to listen and learn more about him and what he might do for them and the whole organization. This does not mean that leaders must be softies. Leadership is about making hard choices. Leaders have to make choices about people, policies, and products, and much more. How they handle those hard decisions that may cause people pain will define their character and set an example that others will remember. Motivation once tapped into is a potent life force that can enable individuals to succeed and organizations to thrive.

## Insights into Motivation: David McClelland

David McClelland, a Harvard psychologist, postulated that managers are motivated by three forces: affiliation, achievement, and power. Managers who have a high degree of affiliation want to be liked. Such managers find it difficult to lead because they do not want to offend or hurt anyone; as a result, affiliative managers find decision making difficult. For managers motivated by achievement, fulfillment comes from getting things done, but they put themselves and their needs first; their goal is to move up the ladder. Managers who are motivated by power enjoy being in control. McClelland, with a colleague, David Burnham, divided managers motivated by power into two subcategories: those who seek personal power and those who seek institutional power. Both types inspire good morale. Personal-power managers develop loyalty to themselves (General George Patton), whereas institutional power managers inspire loyalty to the organization (General Dwight D. Eisenhower).[8]

## Motivation Planner: Exemplify

Setting the right example is the ultimate motivator. It is how people learn behaviors that foster cooperation and teamwork. Use the following questions to begin to see how you can set the right example.

1. Leadership starts inside. Before you can lead others, you must lead yourself. Consider ways in which you can lead from within. Specifically:

- How can you demonstrate autonomy (willingness to be in charge)?
- How can you demonstrate initiative (willingness to make a positive difference)?
- How can you demonstrate responsibility (willingness to be accountable)?

2. Conviction is essential to leadership. Take a moment to describe your values as they relate to
   - Family
   - Friends
   - Work

3. Nothing destroys trust faster than not doing what you say you will do. Reflect on moments when you did not do something that you promised. Why was that? What could you have done differently? What will you do the next time?

4. Compassion is the outward reflection of care and concern for others. Recall examples of leaders that you know who demonstrated compassion. How did they do it? What did you learn from their example? Would you do the same? Why or why not?

5. Leaders are products as well as prodders of their culture. Look at the leadership in your organization. Are your leaders reflecting the organization's vision, mission, and values? If so, why? Are you living the culture? What could you do differently to improve the culture?

## COLONEL DAVID H. HACKWORTH

As the nation girded for war in the late winter of 2003, the cable news channels had kicked into high gear, with round-the-clock coverage of the troop build-up in Kuwait and elsewhere. Among the crowd of reporters and pundits, there was one person who stood out. He had a mop of white hair styled in the manner of Julius Caesar and was dressed in a black crew neck and black sport coat that set off his deep blue eyes, and his commentary was thoughtful and measured. But one night, on CNN's *Larry King Live,* he gave a glimpse of what kind of man he truly was. An anxious mother whose son was stationed in Kuwait as a member of the 101st Airborne, the Screaming Eagles, called in with a question that betrayed her deep concern for her son's safety. Without missing a beat, the commentator smiled and assured that mother that her son was among the best of the best and that he would be fine. In that moment he revealed to the world the soft side of his leadership, which he had developed as a soldier in three wars, including three tours in Vietnam. He is Colonel David H. Hackworth, U.S. Army retired, and the most decorated soldier in U.S. Army history.

## A PRICE ON HIS HEAD

Thirty-five years earlier, the troops he commanded in the Mekong Delta wanted to kill him. In fact, one soldier wrote a letter home to his parents saying that there was a bounty of $1,600 on the colonel's head—and that was just after he arrived.[9] Word also filtered back to headquarters that there was a price on his head. Hack, as his familiars call him, paid it no mind. He had a job to do: to turn this group of green draftees, reluctant warriors, into a fighting force. Why? One, he was under orders to do this, and two, by doing it, he was fulfilling the wish of every man under his command at Firebase Dizzy—to get home safely.[10] So which is the real man—the smiling elder statesman of combat or the hard-nosed disciplinarian? Or is there a third Hackworth, one of the most ardent and vocal voices for America's fighting soldiers? Actually both, or all, are one and the same. David Hackworth comes out of a tradition of fine military commanders who insist on strict discipline, rigorous training, and skillful tactics, all tied together in a single thread that weaves its way through their life: "Take care of the troops."

To understand David Hackworth, you have to delve into his background. At 15 he lied about his age and enlisted in the army, and ended up in Italy at the end of World War II. He stayed in the army and moved up through the ranks, serving time in Korea, and all the while he was honing his knowledge of military strategy and tactics in three ways: on the job, through schooling, and by reading the military classics—most importantly, Sun Tzu's *Art of War*. Anyone who reads Sun Tzu realizes that for all its wisdom concerning strategy and tactics, *Art of War* is really about avoiding war—but if you have to fight, doing it right, with a minimum of casualties. Maneuver over mauling; tactics over excess bloodletting. This is preface to the essence of the man as commander. If you want to gain real insight into Hack as a man and a leader, you can find it in *Steel My Soldiers' Hearts*, a memoir of his third tour in Vietnam. It is more than a turnaround story; it is a virtual handbook on motivation.

## TURNING THINGS AROUND

Things have to be bad before you can turn them around. And at Firebase Dizzy, things were bad. For starters, the firebase was located in the delta, on flat ground that was at or below sea level. It was open and hard to protect—exactly the opposite of what Sun Tzu, as Hackworth points out, would have called for. The previous commander had tried to be a nice guy, but all his niceness had led to was lack of good military order and high casualties; 28 soldiers had been killed in the year prior to Hack's arrival. One sergeant who served under Hackworth but was there first was able years later to recall the names of all the troops in his unit who had died. His wife wondered how he could remember them, to which he replied, "How could I forget?" Adding to this was the growing sentiment that the war was not worth fighting. It was not without reason that the battalion was nicknamed "Hopeless." Yes, the situation was bad.[11]

So what was first thing Hackworth did upon assuming command? He became the toughest, meanest SOB he could be. His orders did not fall on welcome ears. Draftee soldiers in 1969 did not take kindly to officers trying to play tough. But they were wrong. Hack was not playing at anything; he was for real. He insisted on discipline first and began with simple steps. He reinstituted saluting, to which he asked soldiers to respond by saying, "Hardcore Recondo, sir!" To which officers replied, "No slack, soldier."[12] What this did was remind his soldiers that they could be tough, they could be hardcore, and they might survive. He taught them how, beginning with the "two rules a day" concept.[13] The first rule was to keep the weapon clean, and the second was to wear the steel helmet. Clean weapons are weapons that can fire; steel helmets protect against falling shrapnel. He also refused to allow his men to sleep on top of the bunkers; it was cooler there, but it was also highly dangerous. Shortly afterward, the troops came under heavy mortar attack. There were no injuries, and there were few complaints afterward about wearing helmets and sleeping in bunkers.

"The main thing with my school of leadership is to set the example," Hackworth said in an interview. "Let the soldiers know your main concern is their welfare. And in this case, they were facing the ultimate challenge of welfare, that is, their lives being destroyed. . . . [M]y job was to impress upon them that I was going to keep [them] alive, by teaching them to fight the enemy and to win over the enemy. And to do that you had to set the example." Hack is very specific about what it means to set the right example: "You go and lead and let each soldier know that your basic concern is that soldier. You are the first one up, the last one in bed, the last one in the chow line. Once [soldiers] realized that [my] only concern was their welfare, and of course the accomplishment of the mission, it was a piece of cake."[14] Within eight weeks, the Hopeless Battalion became the Hardcore Battalion—alert, capable, and destructive to the enemy.

## TRAINING REGIMEN
And more rules, in the form of training, were added to the regimen. What Hackworth did was train his soldiers on the base and in the field. "Close combat allows little time to think," writes

Hackworth. "Do it right in training and you'll do it right when the incoming slugs flash by."[15] Most importantly, Hack trained right alongside his men. Unlike others of his rank, who hovered high above in helicopters, Hackworth was a ground commander, at one with the grunts. He pushed them hard. "You can't make a unit proud by praising it and you can't make a soldier proud by telling him how tough or good he is," writes Hackworth. "They had to earn it."[16] There was method to what some might have perceived as madness in the sweltering humidity, and it is the second-oldest lesson in command: "If you take care of your soldiers, they will take care of you."[17] The oldest lesson is: "Take care of your soldiers."

Of course, not everyone was thrilled with the regimen. When informed by his commanding general that there was a price on his head, Hack asked what it was. When told that it was $3,500 (up from the original $1,600), Hackworth laughed, asking to be informed when the bounty hit $10,000.[18] After all, Hack says he loves "bitchers." For a commander in a combat zone, this is not false bravado; it's common sense. If things get too quiet, there could be serious trouble.[19] As Colin Powell has put it, a commander who does not hear problems has a problem. In most American wars, and even in today's struggle in Iraq, the troops consist of citizen-soldiers, who Hack believes "are not afraid to get in your face"; he calls them the "heart and soul of the U.S. Army." To win their hearts, a commander has to lead from the front. "[T]he very core of leadership has always been to set the example and let soldiers see that their leaders care about them, share the same risks and conditions."[20] That meant that Hackworth walked the perimeter right alongside his troops—a dangerous position for any solider to be in during a guerrilla war.

## SHOW CARE
What's more, a commander must show love. Hardcore operated in the Mekong Delta, which meant that it was often wet and muddy. "Immersion foot," a.k.a. "trench foot," was a constant threat. Hackworth instructed his men on techniques for keeping

their feet dry; he sought to get them onto dry ground at least four hours a day. He also let them wear cutoffs—a small gesture, but in the heat and humidity of the delta, it was a godsend.[21] And when the troops came in from the field, he inspected their feet. Hack writes, "When a leader gets down on his knees and looks and touches his men's feet, it delivers a clear message: That the commander cares."[22] Soldiers sense the commitment immediately. Says Hack, "This guy is different from the rest of these folks who are just here to look after themselves. . . . He really does care about us. Once you've won them over to your side, you can go to hell and back and they're going to go with you."[23]

He also made it a practice to talk to each and every replacement coming into his base. Replacement troops are always at a disadvantage; they have not shared the bonding process of troops who have been through training and combat together. But such troops are vital to the total effort; if they are too isolated and do not mix in, they become a danger to themselves as well as to others.[24] Unit cohesion is essential to any fighting force. Soldiers do not fight in the field for abstract causes; they fight for their fellow soldiers. Esprit de corps is essential. Hackworth encouraged it right from the start with "arrowhead pins," special insignia, and even stationery. Small things, yes, but they contribute to morale. As Hack writes, "All this said, we're different, we're not just plain old infantry, we're the best."[25]

Recognition was essential to the turnaround effort. "It's been my experience with soldiers, and I think it's true of anyone, if you tell somebody they are good, that reinforces where they are coming from." Hackworth is very clear on this point. "Nobody wants to be a loser. Everyone wants to be a winner." He applied these lessons to Hardcore as well as other troops he commanded. Instead of "beating up on the men," Hackworth says, "I would use a little Irish blarney to tell them how well they were doing," saying "we got a little bit to go." Bottom line, that positive reinforcement "motivated them to get there."[26] Hackworth is always a firm believer in timely recognition. "When you see them doing something right, reward them on the spot. If they did something

really outstanding . . . give them a Bronze Star, [or] an army com-
mendation for valor. Make sure you single them out in front of
their platoon."[27]

There was another benefit to spending time with the men:
information. As he says now, "I have found the greatest problem
with leadership, and I'm not only talking military leadership but
also industrial leadership, it's the top becomes disconnected with
the bottom. So the top has to go down to the very bottom, to the
assembly line, the factory floor, or the fighting element, [to] find
out what his bitches are."[28] Hackworth learned that lesson very
early in his career. His teacher was none other than General
Dwight D. Eisenhower, who had come to visit his reconnaissance
unit in Italy shortly after the end of the war. "How's the chow?"
Ike asked the young Hackworth, who replied, "It stinks. . . . All
we get is Spam." Eisenhower turned to "his general of logistics,
who happened to be in his entourage," and asked why. The logistics man explained that they "had plenty of Spam left from World
War II," to which Ike said, "'Stop that!' And then he poked his fist
in my chest and said, 'Does that take care of it, son?' And I said,
'Yes, sir.' . . . I realized right then that all you had to do was go to
the boss and bitch. . . . I saw him fix this right in front of my
eyes."[29]

Nothing, of course, builds morale more than victories in the
field. And Hardcore had plenty of those. *Steel My Soldiers'
Hearts* contains plenty of action-adventure stories, told with
verve and seat-of-the-pants excitement. But what matters most is
the results: Hardcore put a dent in the enemy and suffered few
casualties under Hack's leadership. To Hack, there is a fine line
between fear and courage. "Confidence, like fear, is contagious.
Troopers can feel it, see it, and smell it—and it will rub off on
soldiers from a platoon to a division. . . . Confidence produces
courage."[30] Confidence comes from something else: a commander who challenges his men to achieve. He raises their expectations, and as a result they perform better than they had thought
they could. That is a key lesson that Hardcore learned, and it is
why so many of them returned home in one piece.

## NEXT PHASE

That was not true for Hackworth—at least psychologically. In January 1971, he gave an interview to a reporter on *ABC News* that was highly critical of the war in Vietnam, and in particular of the army's own effort. Hack cited poor training of troops and a general officer corps that was woefully and willfully out of touch with the reality of the war itself. Going on television was not something that Hackworth took lightly; two factors had pushed him over the edge. One was the promotion to major general of an officer whom Hack knew to be incompetent. The second was Richard Nixon's pardon of Lieutenant William Calley for the massacre at My Lai. These factors, of course, were on top of the three tours of duty that Hack had served in Vietnam. Although he had put in for retirement, the army was not about to let him go gracefully. Despite being a veteran of three wars and the most decorated soldier in U.S. Army history, he was the target of harassment, surveillance, and abuse from the army command. It was a humiliating end to a glorious career.[31]

The army had additional reasons to pursue Hackworth. During his time in Vietnam he had set up a brothel for his troops as well as a drug-treatment program to get soldiers hooked on heroin clean prior to their leaving for the States. Such actions were unorthodox to say the least, but Hackworth argues that he created them for the best of reasons—to take care of his soldiers. The women who worked in the brothel were monitored for venereal diseases and were less likely to pass along the contagion to troops; the soldiers who had heroin habits could get treatment under a physician without fear of punishment. These actions, coupled with his renunciation of the war while on active duty, made Hackworth persona non grata in certain military circles.[32]

Tough soldier and resilient man that he is, Hackworth survived and started his life over in Australia, where he proved to be quite an adept entrepreneur and restaurateur. He wrote his memoirs, *About Face*, which he viewed as a "catharsis" that enabled him to purge himself of ill feelings toward the army that he had bottled up inside himself. The book was widely hailed and became an international best-seller. Its success led him to become a war correspondent; he covered Gulf War I as well as other battles in Bosnia, Kosovo, and Somalia. He publishes a weekly column in *Defense Watch*, which in the spring of 2004 helped to break the story of the prisoner abuse scandals in Abu Ghraib prison in Iraq. For Hackworth, the scandals were echoes of earlier battles he had fought with the military establishment. While Hackworth, like many others, found the soldiers' actions abhorrent, he also found a failure in leadership at the prison and on up the chain.[33]

## VOICE FOR THE GRUNTS

Like all genuine military leaders, at least those with heart, Hack did not, and does not, glory in war. Like Robert E. Lee, who once said, "It is well that war is so terrible, or we should grow too fond of it," Hack is fully cognizant of its intoxication but not under its spell. His writing and reporting depicts the savagery of war—deprivation, suffering, and death—but also the stupidity of bloodshed, especially when it is brought on by incompetent commanders, for whom Hack has no mercy.

In his column and his public appearances, Hack is still fighting for his troops. He is a restless and passionate advocate for America's fighting forces. Hack makes a case for one of his hot-button issues: more training, more armor, and more weaponry—not to mention less political meddling. "We are not going to be a free country," he says, "unless we have a very effective fighting defense shield, and that shield must be held by a soldier who has been trained to a high standard."[34] Aside from his hectoring of the vaunted few—the political and privileged who he feels do not honor their obligation and commitment to America's troops—Hack relentlessly repeats his mantra: "Take care of the troops." Like Winston Churchill, who once quipped that he would be well remembered by history because he intended to write it, Hack's legacy is preserved in his books and columns. But most importantly, and probably more meaningful to him, Hack is well remembered by the troops who served under his command for the example he set as he spoke, taught, delegated, and coached, as well as pushed, prodded, and disciplined—or, in short, *led*. After all, they came home safe. Hack is a soldier's soldier, and among fighting men, there is no higher honor.

## Lessons in Leadership Motivation

- *Prepare your people.* David Hackworth trained his people in body, mind, and spirit. He drilled them in tactics, explained what he was doing and why, and built esprit de corps.

- *Take care of the troops.* Good officers are taught to take care of their men. David Hackworth took care of his men by educating and training them as well as coaching and counseling them, as soldiers and as men.

- *Instill discipline.* No army can function without strict discipline. David Hackworth used discipline to instill order, prepare his troops, and fight aggressively. Discipline also enabled more of his men to return home in one piece.

- *"Inspect the feet."* Hackworth did the little things, like inspecting their feet and engaging them in conversation, to make certain that his men knew that he cared about them.

- *Advocate for your people.* David Hackworth has devoted his post-military career to promoting the rights and security of soldiers in the U.S. military. His passionate advocacy demonstrates to soldiers that someone is looking out for them.

- *Keep your ear to the ground.* The best information comes from the people closest to the action. David Hackworth listened to and learned from his troops, a

(*Continued on next page.*)

lesson he learned directly from General Eisenhower.

- *Learn from the best.* David Hackworth is a student of military history and strategy, in particularly Sun-Tzu's *Art of War*. He disseminates what he has learned in his teaching and his writing.

- *Lead from the front.* David Hackworth never asked his men to do what he himself would not do. He served on the front lines and in the action throughout his military career.

C H A P T E R

3

"People want to feel that what they do makes a difference."

*Frances Hesselbein*
*CEO, Leader to Leader Institute*

"The intention of listening is to restore communication, because once communication is restored, everything is possible."

*Thich Nhat Hanh*
*Author/peace activist*

# COMMUNICATE

## TWO VOICES

*T*HE HISTORY OF IRELAND *is peopled with a number of heroic figures who loom large over the landscape of that troubled island. Sadly, most were martyred in the pursuit of ending tyranny. Add to this list Veronica Guerin, the crusading* *crime reporter for Ireland's* Sunday Independent, *who was gunned down as she waited at a traffic light. Her killing was ordered by drug lords eager to rid themselves of a pesky reporter who refused to surrender to their intimidation.*

*Veronica Guerin began her writing career in public relations. Later, she turned her talents to exposing the underworld. Like many in Ireland, she was outraged that hard drugs, and with them violent crime, were finding their way into middle-class Ireland.[1] Her articles won acclaim, but also enmity. In 1994, the windows of her home were shot out. In 1995, she was shot in the thigh. Later that same year, she was beaten by a convicted criminal, who called her the next day and threatened harm to her young son. Her newspaper and the police offered to provide security, but she begged off, saying that police protection would hinder her investigative efforts. When released from the hospital, she said, "I vow that the eyes of justice, the eyes of this journalist will not be shut again. No hand can deter me from my battle for truth."[2]*

*It was not only the truth that fired up Guerin; it was also the thrill of the chase. "I would, and do, take risks," she once said. "I would meet anyone, do anything to get a story. I'm a newshound. There are great opportunities out there for hungry news hounds—and I am hungry."[3] Her hunger fed a public that was hungry for news about crime. One retired detective (and source for Guerin) put it this way: "Everybody read Veronica Guerin. Everybody throughout the length and breadth of Ireland who wanted to know what was happening went to the Veronica Guerin column, because it was undiluted."[4]*

*Guerin was shot dead on June 26, 1996, just two days before she was to address a conference in London; ironically, the theme of the conference was "Dying to Tell a Story: Journalists at Risk." Her death provoked an uproar. The Irish prime minister, John Bruton, called her death "an attack on democracy." Editors from Ireland and Great Britain issued a joint statement: "Veronica Guerin was murdered for being a journalist. She was a brave and brilliant reporter who was gunned down for being tenacious.*

*This assassination is a fundamental attack on the free press. Journalists will not be intimated."*[5]

As a result of her death, Irish police brought down the hammer on Irish organized crime. Her killers were imprisoned for life, as were those who ordered her killed. Two movies have been made of her life. A judge who conducted a trial of one of her killers concluded his judgment with these words: *"To those who grieve for the late Ms. Guerin, the Court would like to say that by her death she contributed immeasurably to the successful identification and destruction of this drug importation and distribution enterprise. Hopefully this will have spared many young people from the scourge of drugs. If this is so, then her death will not have been in vain."*[6] Veronica Guerin's legacy is that truth can prevail over crime when that truth is backed by the courage and moral conviction of a reporter willing to risk her life.

*When he was presented with a gold medal from President John F. Kennedy for "services to his nation," he deadpanned, "I feel very humble," followed by the classic line, "But I think I have the strength of character to fight it."* That was Bob Hope, ever the crackup even on the most solemn occasions.

And why not? Here was a guy who played a character in a movie who was asked if he was afraid—to which he shot back, *"Not me. I was in vaudeville."* He could have been speaking about himself. Born in London, Hope emigrated to Cleveland with his parents at the age of four. His first profession was prizefighting. *"Some fighters are carried to their dressing rooms, I'm the only one they carried both ways."* He graduated to vaudeville, another highly competitive arena. He traveled relentlessly, often doing four shows a day. It was the way he learned his craft.

Upon his death at age 100, many of his costars recalled working with him. Some noted his singing voice; others his ability to dance. He was a pretty fair singer and hoofer. But his gift was comedy. He had a crackling wit, and although he employed

*teams of writers, whom he credited, it was really Hope who made
their lines come to life. Said Mel Shavelson, "We took his own
characteristics and exaggerated them. The woman chaser. The
coward. The cheap guy. We just put them in. He thought he was
playing a character. He was playing, really, the real Bob Hope."*

*And it was the real Bob Hope who struck a chord with GIs
stationed far from home. From World War II through the first Gulf
War, one constant was Bob Hope at Christmas. Detractors said
he did it for the applause. Of course he did, but to travel tens of
thousands of miles year after year to hostile territories took more
than a desire for laughs. It was a commitment to men and women
and the nation that he had embraced as his own. Hope was not a
rear-line comedian; he went as close to the front as they would let
him. Once in Vietnam an enemy sniper was killed just before his
performance. In Saigon, after an officer's billet was blown up, he
joked, "I was on my way to the hotel and I passed a hotel going
the opposite direction." He also got down to basics in Vietnam.
"Technically we're not at war," he joked in 1966, "so remember
that when you get shot: Technically, it doesn't hurt." Hope himself
suffered in Vietnam; he was viewed by some as a propagandist for
the political and military establishment, and soldiers booed him
on occasion. He could not understand; he had come to cheer
them up, but they had stood him up. Even vaudeville was not so
cruel.*

*Despite the catcalls in Vietnam, Bob Hope had special ties to
the ranks. Many thousands wrote to him telling him where they
had seen him and what it had meant to them when he showed up,
often in some god-forsaken place that no one would ever want to
visit, especially at Christmas. No one except Bob Hope, that is,
often bringing with him a bevy of beautiful women as singers,
dancers, and, of course, props for his act. The legacy of Bob
Hope lives on in his many Road pictures, recordings of his radio
shows, and tapes of his hundreds of television specials. But for
many Americans, the real Bob Hope lives on in their memories,
apt perhaps for an entertainer whose theme song was "Thanks
for the Memories."*

*Perhaps it will strike some as odd that we are looking to a comedian for inspiration, but upon further reflection, who better to look to than someone who makes us laugh? And when it comes to Bob Hope, the legacy of his long life is service to others in the pursuit of making people happy, whether they were in living rooms in Cleveland or Seattle or watching on makeshift stands in France, Korea, Vietnam, or a hundred others places in between. Bob Hope loved what he did, and he made others enjoy it, too.*[7]

⁓⊙ ⊙⁓

"No news is good news" is a mantra that echoes in every workplace. Many of us are so conditioned to hearing only complaints from our bosses that we treat silence from on high as a positive. When lack of communication is considered to be a good thing, managers are not doing a good job of articulating the organization's message or listening to what people have to say. As a result, they are missing a huge opportunity to motivate. Communication is an expression of a leader's sincerity and conviction.

As a leader, how you communicate is essential to how you lead. Leaders who do not communicate cannot lead. Communication is more than articulating a message. It involves creating a relationship that is based upon trust in order to achieve intended and inspired results. Veronica Guerin built trust by her reporting in the pursuit of organized crime; Bob Hope built trust by puncturing the powers that be in the pursuit of laughter. Both achieved results through the honesty of their voice and the integrity of their work.

## FORGING A RELATIONSHIP

Your followers need direction from their leaders about where they are headed, what they need to do to get there, and how they will know when they have arrived. They need to know the large-scale context (where the organization is headed) as well as the personal context (what do I do today and why do I do it?). That is where leadership comes in. Leaders use their communications to inform, but also, more importantly, to build a relationship, a sense that "I will show you the way." People will follow their leaders only if they trust them. Trust begins with communication, telling the truth and being clear and direct with people. It is fortified by example, doing what is right and what is good for people and the organization. When your people trust you, they will do what you ask of them, and together you will achieve the goals and the results for which you are striving.

Sad to say, however, most companies are not perceived to be good communicators. A survey taken in the spring of 2004 by Maritz Market Research showed that only 7 percent of employees rated their companies as doing a good job of communicating; 44 percent said they were doing a poor job. According to Rick Garlick, Ph.D., a director at Maritz, these figures also applied to the senior leaders of these companies: few were perceived as "acting consistently with their words."[8]

Communication is an action step, and, like all actions, it must be evaluated. A good way to evaluate your communication is to listen to your people. But you do not simply listen; you check for understanding. As a leader, you must forever be asking, do people understand what they are supposed to do? The answer to that question can be found in the behavior of your people and in the work they do. If they are following your positive example and doing what needs to be done, the question has been answered. If this is not occurring, you need to keep asking the same question. And even when things are going well, you never stop asking questions and you never stop communicating.

Communication is integral to leadership, so much so that leaders must practice it at every level of the organization. Leaders must find opportunities to speak, to listen, and to learn from others—from the shop floor to the top floor. Communication is the way in which leaders build the relationships they need in order to enable their people to fulfill personal, team, and organizational goals.

As a manager, you are the living face of the organization to your people. How you lead them will determine your success and theirs. As a leader, you are responsible for unleashing the creativity and energy of your people and your team. As a leader, you are not simply creating followers, you are creating future leaders. This is a significant responsibility, but a rewarding one. These men and women will build upon what you have done and produce even greater results for the organization, for the team, and for themselves.

## QUEST FOR AUTHENTICITY

So just what is communication? An articulation of a message? A conversation? A relationship? It is all of these things and more. It is a process by which two or more people connect on a level that binds them together. Connection is a root of leadership; it is founded on authenticity, the soul of who you are as a leader. Your authenticity is your character, which is made up of your beliefs and values along with your commitment to your organization. Authenticity is readily apparent to those who work with you; it is how they picture you.

For a leader, then, communication is the act of making authenticity transparent. You can achieve this transparency in three ways: speaking, listening, and learning. The essence of leadership communication boils down to this three-step cycle, which is in perpetual motion. Not only is the cycle always moving, but at any given time, you will find yourself in one of the steps with some person. At one point you will be speaking to a colleague. At another time you will be listening to a group. And at yet another time you will be in your office or in your home thinking about what you heard and trying to make sense of it.

Leaders need to communicate through words, thoughts, and actions. Leaders need to iterate their messages, listen for feedback, and act for the organization. When communications are clear and honest, motivation can occur. Thich Nhat Hanh was exiled from his Vietnamese homeland for advocating peace in time of war. Rather than giving up, he became more outspoken in his writings as well as his personal example. He lives simply as a monk and imparts his wisdom through conversation, books, and prayer.

## SPEAK AS A LEADER

Articulating the message is the first step in the cycle. It initiates the leadership relationship when the leader is new, and renews it regularly as the leader guides the organization. When John F. Kennedy delivered his inaugural address in January 1961, he articulated his nation's commitment to the cause of ensuring freedom throughout the world. His "bear any burden" phrase sent a clear message that the United States was serious about its intentions. And he challenged the American people to do their part when he said, "Ask not what your country can do for you— ask what you can do for your country." As it did for Kennedy, speaking gives you the opportunity to put your best foot forward and to invite people to participate in your effort.

- *Adopt the leadership mindset.* Good leadership begins with an assumption of command, that is, responsibility for leading others. It is centered within a strong sense of self and a commitment to personal leadership. Personal leadership is composed of three elements: autonomy (willingness to be in charge), initiative (willingness to make a positive difference), and responsibility (willingness to be accountable) (see Chapter 2). With a foundation of personal leadership, you are able to lead others. Leadership is the process of achieving results for and by the efforts of others in order to make things better for individuals, teams, and organizations. Some leadership decisions involve short-term pain, e.g., promoting one person over another, closing a business, or laying off workers. But such deci-

sions must be made with the whole organization in mind.
Leadership messages emerge from this leadership mindset.

- *Align your message.* Leadership messages should reflect
  the vision, mission, and strategies of the organization. The
  leader's chief responsibility is to get others to follow. Part
  of this process involves getting those people aligned
  behind what the organization needs to do and how it needs
  to do it. For example, a social service agency that provides
  temporary shelter for the homeless must provide beds,
  food, and other forms of assistance. People who work or
  volunteer for the agency need to know what it means to
  serve the poor as well as how to do it tactically, e.g., provide adequate bedding, offer nutritious food, and create a
  safe environment. Messages from the leader of the agency
  reinforce this mission.

- *Refresh your message.* Much of leadership communication is iteration and reiteration. Repetition reinforces what
  you say and adds significance to the message. But even
  important messages can become stale. It is important to
  keep them fresh. A good way to do this is through stories.
  For example, if you are in the middle of a transformation,
  note success stories that mark important milestones. Best
  practices that emerge from change are also good things
  for people to know. When such things are incorporated
  into the message, they not only keep it fresh but they
  make it more credible. People will say, "We are making
  progress, after all."

- *Give feedback.* People want to know where they stand and
  what the organization needs from them. Leaders owe it to
  their people to provide honest feedback. While feedback
  is typically considered part of the listening process, and it
  is, it can also be part of the speaking process if you take
  this approach. Compliment people on what they are doing
  right and follow up by asking what you can do to help
  them do it better.

## LISTEN FOR UNDERSTANDING

So much of communication focuses on speaking, the articulation of thoughts, that we tend to overlook the next step in the cycle, listening. When we consider good leaders, we tend naturally to think of those who could articulate a message. Equally important, however, is the ability to listen. Mohandas Gandhi is a good example of a listener. Gandhi was a barrister by training, but when he became involved in the cause of Indian independence, he adopted a more contemplative way of life. He listened to those around him, even, very importantly, those who opposed him, including the British, the Muslims, and more radical Hindus. His message of nonviolent resistance emerged from listening; it was an active, not a passive, step. A good way for leaders to become better listeners is to consider listening to be an active step. It opens the door for people to know that you care.

- *Ask questions.* Leaders need to know what is going on. A natural sense of curiosity is healthy, and you exercise it by asking questions. These questions will help the leader be informed and stay in the loop, as well as initiate a relationship between leader and follower. When people come to understand that their leader wants to know what they do, it demonstrates personal commitment to what they do.

- *Probe for details.* How people respond to a first question may not reveal the whole answer. It is up to the leader to ask follow-up questions that begin with why and how. These open-ended questions will open the door to conversation. When you are probing, however, it is important for you to be honest, but to hold yourself in check if you learn bad news. You may feel like blowing your stack, but if you do, you may destroy trust. People need to know that they can come to you with bad news as well as good news.

- *Employ brief-back techniques.* Invite people to tell you what you have told them and what they will do about it. Brief-back is a technique employed by the military to ensure understanding. The one giving the briefing asks his subordinates what has been said and how they will do what has been asked. For example, if a colonel tells a lieutenant to move his squad to another sector, the lieutenant will reiterate what he's been ordered to do and provide details, as much as he can, about how he will do it in terms of troops, armaments, and supplies.

## LEARN FROM WHAT YOU SEE AND HEAR

The leadership process is about achieving results, of course, but since those results come chiefly through and by others, it is important that a leader always try to work for those others' best interests. The learning part of the leadership communication cycle is a way to demonstrate how important people are to the process of getting things done. Learning also becomes proof that you have listened. The Japanese management culture is steeped in a concept known as "tacit knowledge." Tacit knowledge is the knowledge of what you need to do in order to get things done. It is gained not from books but from watching others and from personal experience. Putting what you observe into practice is a good way to demonstrate what you have learned. When employees see their leaders adopting their ideas, it tells them that they must be doing something right, a good motivator in itself.

- *Reflect on what you have heard.* The learning part of the leadership communication cycle can really work only if you process what you sense through conversation and observation. By reflecting—that is, by thinking back on what you have said, what kind of feedback you have received, and how people have reacted emotionally—you gain a sense of perspective. And if you think hard enough, you will learn how you can make your messages stronger and more aligned with the organization's needs as well as how you can be more responsive to the needs of your people. Setting aside some time each day to reflect is a good practice, but the thoughts encouraged by this practice will strike you at any time of day.

- *Consider what you have observed but not heard.* Often what is not said may be more important than what is said. For example, if a manager passes by an employee and asks him how things are going, and the employee responds, "Fine," in a listless tone while looking down at his feet, you can bet that he is not telling all he knows. He may be hiding details out of fear. Studies from the Gallup organization show that far too often, fear is a leading sentiment among employees, and with good reason. Our management culture punishes or ignores more than it rewards. Therefore, it is up to the leader to read body language, sense the mood of teams, and gauge the sentiment of the organization. You can do this by walking around and being accessible, as well as through focus groups and surveys.

- *Plot your next steps.* The process of achieving results requires actions that are fed by communication. Thoughts stimulated by reflection and observation will guide you in the development of future messages. This will also be your opportunity to incorporate the thinking of others into your process. No leader is an island; she needs the support of others. This is not a form of retreat or weakness; it is an opportunity to grow and develop.

## ACT ON WHAT YOU HAVE LEARNED

What you do with what you have learned will determine your success as a leader. When leaders incorporate some or all of what they have learned into their next round of messages, they demonstrate that they are not working in a vacuum, but rather are taking the needs of others into consideration. When a leader is pushing transformational initiatives, resistance always occurs, but sometimes this resistance will lessen when employees perceive that their wishes are being considered. Often people ask only for a voice. Your actions in the speak-listen-learn cycle demonstrate that they have a voice, and that it is being heard. As a CEO and eloquent essayist, Frances Hesselbein puts her thoughts and writings into practice as she focuses on mission, innovation, and diversity, and by doing so, she brings the organization and the people in it into a new tomorrow. Like all good leaders, Hesselbein learns as she goes and shares those lessons with us.

How well you practice the three-step cycle will go a long way toward determining your effectiveness as a motivator. By practicing it regularly and consistently, you will be providing people with direction, allowing them a voice in what you do, and, very importantly, learning with and from them. While the cycle of speaking, listening, and learning is perpetual, at any given time, you will find yourself in one of the steps of the process. Taken as a whole, this is a powerful process that not only keeps you and your people informed but creates a bond between you and your people that is rooted in trust and nurtured by inspired results.

## Insights into Motivation: Fredrick Herzberg

Fredrick Herzberg, a behavioral psychologist who studied motivation in the workplace, developed the "motivation-hygiene" theory. It divides motivation into two categories, intrinsic factors relating to the individual and extrinsic factors related to the workplace. Intrinsic factors include "achievement, recognition for achievement, the work itself, responsibility, and growth or advancement." Extrinsic factors ("hygiene") include "company policy and administration, supervision, interpersonal relationships, working conditions, salary, status, and security." What Herzberg discovered is that what's inside matters more than what's outside. That is, we derive our motivation from ourselves—our need to achieve. However, while extrinsic factors, such as compensation and working conditions, do contribute to job satisfaction when they are good, they destroy job satisfaction when they are poor. Herzberg's thinking led to the development of job enrichment, which "provides opportunity for the employee's psychological growth." This theory influences how human resource departments structure work and career development plans, providing opportunities for employees to assume greater levels of autonomy, responsibility, and authority as they progress through the management ranks.[9]

## Motivation Planner: Communication

Communication is essential for understanding, the foundation of good motivation. Use the following questions to help you structure your communication efforts to foster good motivation.

Review the leadership communication cycle. Think about how you can make it come to life in your regular communications.

### Speaking as a Leader

- How do you articulate the leadership mindset, i.e., what the organization is doing and why?
- How do you align your messages with the organization? What processes do you use, e.g., presentations, meetings, conversations, e-mail, and so on?
- How do you keep your messages fresh? Do you tell stories about what your people are doing to help boost morale and encourage best practices? Explain.
- How regularly do you give feedback to your people?

---

## Listening for Understanding

- How do you use questions to demonstrate your interest?
- How do you let people know that you want to know more about what they do?
- How do you ensure understanding with brief-backs? Do you use brief-backs after meetings or coaching sessions?

## Learning from What You See and Hear

- How much time do you set aside each day (or week) to ponder what you have seen and heard?
- What have you seen, but not heard? That is, what do you think people are not telling you, and why?
- Based upon what you have seen and heard, what do you plan to do next?

---

## FRANCES HESSELBEIN

In 1976, there were rumors that the Boy Scouts were considering recruiting younger girls to join their organization; they had already opened their doors to teenage girls. Why? Because at that time the management of the Girl Scouts of the USA was in disarray, and there were fears that the organization might disintegrate. Today, a generation later, the Girl Scouts are the model of what a nonprofit organization can be, and its leadership practices are widely emulated by organizations in the for-profit sector. Much of the credit for the turnaround can be given to Frances Hesselbein, who headed the Girl Scouts for 13½ years beginning in the middle seventies. Hesselbein would object to the term *headed*; as CEO of Girl Scouts of the USA, she viewed herself as being at the center of the organization. As she once explained to a reporter for

*Business Week*, leaders are at the center of a series of concentric circles of people and responsibility. A centrally positioned leader acts as a nexus of information and responsibility that she can leverage to serve the needs of individuals and the organization. This leadership model, which Hesselbein calls "circular management," is grounded in character and principle and is a highly motivational mode of management.[10]

## LESSONS OF WESTERN PENNSYLVANIA

Hesselbein's spirit of volunteerism reaches back to her upbringing in the mountains of western Pennsylvania. "When I was growing up it was big steel, big coal, big labor, big hearts. . . . It was a diverse community where people came from all over the world to work in the steel mills and coal mines. It was an extremely generous community that cared about all its children." As a wife and mother, she helped her husband, John, build his career in communications, but she also carved out a niche for herself in volunteer work. She became the first woman to chair the United Way campaign. "There was great consternation. 'Can women really raise money?'" she laughs as she recalls the story. Not to worry. With the backing of Bethlehem Steel and the steelworkers' union (USWA), "we involved the whole community. Little Johnstown, Pennsylvania, that year had the highest per capita giving of any United Way in the United States." As a volunteer leader, she learned two valuable lessons: how to "mobilize a community" and how to "bring people together and be passionate around a mission." The principal focus of her volunteerism was the Girl Scouts, beginning as leader of Troop 17. As she says now, Johnstown "was a marvelous place to understand that leadership is an adventure. My early management lessons I learned right there as a community volunteer."[11]

She leveraged those lessons wisely. She did such an exemplary job that after six years as CEO of two Pennsylvania Girl Scout councils, she moved to New York to become CEO of the national organization, Girl Scouts of the USA. "Everything in my life seems by accident," she laughs. "I found myself CEO of the largest organization for girls and women in the world," even though she had "never applied, nor would have thought of applying for the job."[12]

Hesselbein's humility is one way in which she connects to her people. She always thinks of herself as one of them, another volunteer or staff member. But along the way, she had honed another valuable skill—the ability to communicate effectively. She had worked with her husband to support his career in the communications business, first as an editor and later as a film-maker. "I thought of it as helping John. It never occurred to me that sometime in the future I would have a career where every-thing I ever learned about communications would be very, very helpful."[13] Frances Hesselbein is an eloquent speaker and a good storyteller. Her voice modulates with the drama of the story, and you can hear the charm and warmth in her voice. Her vocabulary resonates with respect words and courtesies that underscore the fact that she regards people as human beings, not just names.

## THE DRUCKER CONNECTION

When she speaks of Peter Drucker, the esteemed management teacher, author, and philosopher as well as her friend and mentor, you can perceive the full range of her storytelling abilities. She first met Drucker at a dinner at New York University held for presidents of foundations and volunteer organizations. She arrived at the appointed hour, and she was the first to arrive. "I turned around and behind me there was a man. 'I am Peter Drucker. Obviously if you grow up in Vienna, 5:30 is 5:30,'" she recalls, her voice dropping an octave to mimic the great man's baritone. Drucker had caught Hesselbein by surprise, but it was she who provided the bigger surprise. "Do you realize how important you are to the Girl Scouts?" she asked. He replied, "No, tell me."[14]

And she did, telling him how all of the 335 Girl Scout coun-cils had copies of his books on their shelves and, better yet, had put them to good use. She told Drucker, "'If you look at our new corporate planning, corporate management system, you will see your philosophy expressed there.' He said, 'You're very daring. I would be afraid to do that. Tell me, does it work?' And I said, 'It works remarkably well.'" And it has continued to work. For the next eight years, Drucker studied the organization, advised the national board and staff, and wrote and spoke widely about how well run the Girl Scouts were His message was all the more authoritative because, in addition to being the father of modern management, he spent much of his time, as Hesselbein says, studying volunteers at the grassroots level.[15]

## GIRL SCOUT LEADERSHIP

When Hesselbein first became CEO of the Girl Scouts, it was a time of great transition. Her first task was critical: She listened to people at all levels of the organization. She also posed a question. "I wanted to know how our people who worked, whether volunteers or staff, how would they describe the organization?" The answers were varied: "a program for girls organization . . . a women's organization . . . [and] a community-based organization." While the comments were laudable, they were not in harmony. As Hesselbein explains, "I thought, if all of us aren't singing out from the same page of the same hymn book, how can we be focused?" So together with her team, Hesselbein defined the new organization as "mission focused, values based, and demographics driven." That means, "We managed for the mission. We managed for innovation. We managed for diversity. . . . We had a very clear answer" for the new organization.[16]

Hesselbein distilled Juliette Lowe's 1912 statement of purpose, which she describes as "very long" and "beautiful," into these words: "'Help each girl reach her own highest potential.' So there was no confusion about what business we were in. Why we were an organization. Why we did what we did. And that was the mission statement that we used at that time." Very importantly, this new mission statement galvanized the spirit of the renewed organization. "We could remember it; and . . . it said what we fervently believed: to help each girl reach her own highest potential." Words became powerful motivators.[17]

## EVERYONE'S INCLUDED

Inclusion is big to Hesselbein. As the leader of the Girl Scouts, she needed to reinvigorate the organization. But not at the expense of its values. "If I am a Navajo child on a reservation, a newly arrived Vietnamese child, or a young girl in rural Appalachia, I have be able to open [the *Girl Scout Handbook*] and find myself there." Hesselbein adds, "That's a very powerful message that 'I'm not an outsider. I'm part of something big.'"[18] Hesselbein pushed the Girl Scouts into the modern age by embracing diversity but also by providing educational materials in core subjects like math and computer science as well as on life issues like teen pregnancy. As Jim Collins, the eminent leadership scholar and author, says, "Hesselbein grasped a central paradox of change: the organizations that best adapt to a changing world first and foremost know what should *not* change." Get the guiding principles right and you can change everything else.[19] In other words, character and values are central; situations dictate movement.

## CIRCULAR MANAGEMENT

Hesselbein's concept of circular management is a form of inclusion. The CEO resides in the center of three concentric circles, each containing core staff and functions. The advantage of this centeredness is lateral movement; a leader can assemble teams quickly and effectively. "Moving across the organization and giving people an opportunity to work with others in different ways, I find, generates marvelous energy and enthusiasm." What's more, the old language of top, down, superior, and subordinate dissolves. As she explains, "Not only do you get superior results, superior performance, there is something about not having language that contains us, and it's a very powerful dimension."[20]

When a leader's constituents surround her, it leads to the elimination of "turf battles, the star system, and the Lone Ranger." Instead, centeredness contributes to partnership. For nonprofits, partnerships will be varied constituencies— "corporations, government agencies, and social sector organizations."

The way to manage properly is to learn to manage to three priorities: mission, innovation, and diversity. Hesselbein sums up these priorities as knowing what you do, ensuring flexibility, and managing for inclusion of people and priorities.[21]

As much as Hesselbein focuses on others (hence the concept of circular management), like all good leaders, she believes that her place is at the front. As she urges, "Lead from the front, don't push from the rear." Toward that end, leaders must be seen and heard articulating the mission, vision, and values of the organization. Or, as Hesselbein puts it, "Leaders model desired behaviors, never break a promise, and know that leadership is a matter of how to be, not how to do it."[22]

The concept of a leader "being" is integral to Hesselbein, but as a student of leadership, she understands that being is not enough. Leadership, after all, is about doing. So she has come up with the concept of "how to be." Drawing a contrast with management by analysis, Hesselbein argues that leaders should focus their "how" on people. As she says, organizations need leaders who are "focused on *how to be*—how to develop quality, character, mind-set, values, principles, and courage." Such leaders will be the ones that people follow; these will be the leaders that inspire loyalty.[23]

## LEADING BY EXAMPLE

"You can't just talk your values," says Hesselbein. "Your people watch you. . . . Everything you do should be the embodiment of what you say you believe and what you do believe."[24] Hesselbein believes that consistency with values is essential. "[I]t's very disillusioning when they hear [their] leader talking about how people are their greatest asset then they treat [their people] solely as cost. It does nothing to motivate people. But when the leader's language and behavior are consistent with the values the leader preaches, it's amazing how liberating that is for people."[25] At the same time, leaders have to make tough choices, often about people. According to Hesselbein, "Not everyone can fit into the organization. Drucker's advice is, '[Y]ou should re-pot them.'" It is the leader's responsibility to "match the person to the demands [and] the opportunities of the position." Keeping someone in a position for which he is ill suited is "futile and unfair to all the other people."[26]

## ELOQUENT COMMUNICATOR

Hesselbein writes about leadership with striking clarity. In one memorable essay, "Carry a Big Basket," she connects a bit of folk wisdom she heard as a young Girl Scout troop leader with her affinity for baskets. The advice was, "You have to carry a big basket to bring something home." Hesselbein uses the basket as a metaphor for transporting new ideas, values, opportunities for others, and her "mission focus." As Hesselbein writes, "What we carry in our basket and what we bring home can change lives and build community. It can transform the organization and the society." The influence of the basket does not end with others, concludes Hesselbein. "[W]e ourselves are transformed."[27] In another essay, "The Power of Civility," Hesselbein discusses the need for manners, something she feels has been compromised. "Leadership is all about valuing relationships, about valuing people." Therefore, common courtesies like standing up when "someone enters our office" or not looking "at our watch when we are talking" are important. "Real etiquette is not about mindless, or archaic ritual; it is about the quality and character of who we are." Such etiquette demonstrates "genuine respect for others and for the tasks we share." Hesselbein may employ metaphor in her language, but her values are as clear and evident as her consistent and persistent focus on people as people.[28]

One way in which Hesselbein stays connected to her people is by listening. This is something she learned from her grandmother in Pennsylvania, whom she credits as being her greatest influence. Her grandmother was a good listener. For Hesselbein, listening is a form of connection. She explains that effective listening requires "total engagement" so that we are heard and understood. Listening affirms "circular communication"; in other words, all parties participate and therefore have a stake in the enterprise. Part of listening also involves listening to ourselves. As she puts it so eloquently, "The whispers of our lives are very important. If we ignore them our lives are diminished" because we will have failed to gain self-knowledge.[29] Service to others lies at the core of her leadership, and she reiterates this theme often. "Every person who works for us is a person of great worth and dignity, and they deserve a position description that is the very best that we can develop so it communicates to them how important they are to the organization."[30]

It may not come as a surprise that people cannot say no to Frances Hesselbein. As Jim Collins confesses in the foreword to her book, *Hesselbein on Leadership*, he has come to realize that he will be obliged to say yes to any request from Frances Hesselbein.[31] Like so many other people whom Hesselbein has worked with, Collins knows that her requests emerge from the center of her being. She does not ask for herself, she asks on behalf of someone else or some organization. You cannot say no to someone who is so selfless. As such, Frances Hesselbein is an exemplar of motivation; she gets the right people to do the right things for the right reasons.

## NONPROFIT ENTERPRISE

Hesselbein's world is that of the nonprofits. As chairman of the Leader to Leader Institute (formerly the Drucker Foundation), she is active in the mission of developing others. Quoting Peter Drucker, she says about nonprofits' efforts in the United States, "No matter what the problem, some non-profit organization has found a way to solve it." Hesselbein sees nonprofits as being on the front lines. "One of the greatest skills of non-profit leaders is that they're on the ground in the neighborhoods and in the communities. They understand the needs." And, like Hesselbein, they are pragmatic. The leaders of nonprofits "can find a corporate partner or government agency" to help them solve the problem.[32] Hesselbein also draws a line between "governance and management." Boards of directors determine an organization's vision, mission, and goals; management executes according to those goals.[33] Her pragmatism extends to exit strategies, using a term that Drucker invented, "planned abandonment," which she defines as "a process by which the board examines its policies, practices and procedures, and assumptions, and asks 'Are these relevant for the future, or do these need to be changed?'"[34] Such questions can prevent mission creep and keep the organization focused on the needs of its constituents.

In 1998, Hesselbein was awarded the nation's highest civilian honor, the Presidential Medal of Freedom, by President Bill Clinton. Her citation noted her work with the Girl Scouts and the Peter F. Drucker Foundation for Nonprofit Management. But, true to her spirit, it was also a time of levity. When President Clinton was awarding the medals, he called the honorees up to the stage one at a time. When Hesselbein's turn came, the president paused, then said, "Anyone who knows Frances Hesselbein knows that she does not permit hierarchical language to be used in her presence, [so] I will ask this pioneer for women, diversity, and inclusion, 'Frances, would you please come, not up, please come *forward*.'"[35] She has also been awarded 16 honorary degrees from such institutions as Boston College, Lafayette College, the University of Nebraska, and the University of Pittsburgh. Her work with the Girl Scouts was profiled in a Harvard Business School case study. She also is an active speaker on leadership issues and has addressed many corporate and nonprofit organizations, including Chevron-Texaco, Microsoft, the National Urban League, ServiceMaster, and Toyota, as well as the U.S. Naval Academy at Annapolis and the U.S. Military Academy at West Point.[36]

## FUTURE VISION

One theme that runs through Hesselbein's work is the future. "People are hungry for significance. They're hungry for leadership."[37] Unlike some senior managers, who pay little attention to tomorrow, Hesselbein talks and writes about it frequently. She edited a collection of essays entitled *Leader of the Future*, and she has written many essays on the topic herself. In one memorable essay, "When the Roll Is Called in 2010," Hesselbein presents a checklist of some 30 tasks that must be done in order to prepare for tomorrow. Among her considerations are a periodic review of the organization's mission and the importance of limiting "strategic goals" to five. Very importantly, she notes the need for leadership development and the need for "grooming successors," which she considers "part of the leader's daily challenges." While no one can predict the future, Hesselbein advocates keeping to the mantra of "mission, innovation, and diversity."[38]

Like all visionary leaders, Hesselbein looks ahead to the next challenge. As she says, "I have a vision of the future . . . that is healthy children, all children, strong families, good schools, decent housing, and work that dignifies—all embraced in this cohesive, diverse, inclusive community that cares about all of its people." Hesselbein realizes that this vision is far from completion, and it serves to push her forward. "It's out there before you, inspiring and invigorating."[39] Peter Drucker once told the *New York Times*, "Frances Hesselbein could manage any company in America." High praise from the man who reinvented the practice of management and fitting praise for a leader who leads from the center, guided by her values, her principles, and her people.

---

## Lessons in Leadership Motivation

- *Educate people.* Frances Hesselbein teaches through her example and her writings. Through her, people learn what they can do to make the world a better place.

- *Articulate the values.* As a writer and an editor, Frances Hesselbein presents a view of leadership that is rooted in service to others.

- *Do what you say you will do*. Frances Hesselbein holds herself to high standards and lives her life according to those standards.
- *Embrace diversity*. Frances Hesselbein believes that including people in the mission makes the vision more attainable as well as more meaningful.
- *Manage pragmatically*. Nonprofits will not succeed unless they are well led and well managed. Hesselbein has spent her life demonstrating by example (as well as through her writing) how organizations must be led in order to succeed.
- *Point to the future*. Frances Hesselbein has a vision of the world that includes rather than excludes and affirms the dignity of children and families. She uses this future to invigorate herself and her work.

## THICH NHAT HANH

On the inside flap of one of his books is a collection of quotes from famous people praising either him or his work. Thomas Merton said that he "is more my brother than many who are nearer to me." Robert Lowell called him "a real poet." Martin Luther King referred to him as "a holy man." The Dalai Lama refers to the "connections between personal, inner peace and peace on earth."[40] In a sense, all of these great men saw a reflection of themselves and their values in him—mysticism, poetry, holiness, and connectivity. Thich Nhat Hanh is all of these and more, though if given the choice, he would prefer to be considered as "thay," or teacher.[41]

## MAN OF PEACE

Small in stature, with a radiant smile and wide-open eyes that seem to drink in the world and the people in it, Thich Nhat Hanh is one of the great men of peace in our era. Banished from his home country, Vietnam, during the late sixties, he has become world-renowned as a poet, writer, and teacher. The author of more than 100 books, over 40 in English, Thich Nhat Hanh is someone who inspires by example. As a Buddhist monk, his life is one of connectedness—to self, to community, to the world, to peace. He writes with simplicity and directness, weaving together personal anecdotes, Buddhist parables, and modern-day stories. He also can be scholarly, as in his lengthy book *The Heart of Buddha's Teaching*. In his writing there is a gentility of spirit coupled with things that people can do to make life better for themselves and others.

## ENGAGED BUDDHISM

Thich Nhat Hanh is the founder of a movement begun in the 1950s that he calls Engaged Buddhism. It is Buddhism with a social conscience, or, as he puts it more eloquently, "a product of suffering and war—a lotus flower blooming in a sea of fire." Its intention was to bring the practice of Buddhism to bear on "all areas of life . . . economics, education, and art, among other things."[42] His monks created "self-help villages," modeled after the kibbutzim in Israel, to help the villagers create self-sustaining communities. In 1964, he created the School of Youth for Social Service. By combining the knowledge of social workers with that of farmers, underscored by a commitment to Buddhism, the School of Youth was able to improve four aspects of peasant life: "rural education, health, economics, and organization."[43] Before they were able to do anything, social workers needed to live among the people and experience life from their vantage point. This was how the social workers established trust and were able to proceed with education and health-care services. They also sought to connect to local Buddhist temples and gain their support. Naturally, in this time of war, the school was an object of suspicion on both sides, the communists and the nationalists. There were many casualties.[44]

Thich Nhat Hanh tells the story of one village where six social workers were taken out and killed on orders from the local commandant. The soldiers who did the killing acted under orders, not out of malice. By this time, Thich Nhat Hanh had been exiled from Vietnam and was living in Paris. One of his associates, Sister Chan Khong, organized funerals and read this statement: "Dear friends, you don't understand us, and that is why you have killed us. Our intention is not to do harm to anyone. We only want to help."[45] Such a statement might at first seem naïve, painfully so in the light of the deaths of such good people, but this statement is a reflection of what Thich Nhat Hahn was teaching then and has taught for his entire life—that it is not *people* who are enemies; the enemies are hatred, war, and violence.[46] Later on, Sister Chan, practicing what she had been taught, was able to intercede between American and communist forces during a siege of Saigon in order to evacuate wounded from the campus of the School for Youth.[47]

## DISTILLING HIS MESSAGE

While it would be presumptuous to try to distill what Thich Nhat Hanh teaches into a few sentences, it is possible to echo the core principles that are woven throughout his writings. Like all Buddhists, he acknowledges that Buddha, the goodness, resides in each of us. It is our responsibility to discover or uncover it. We do this through becoming mindful in our vision, our thinking, and our actions. Communication is essential to mindfulness, and it manifests itself in a number of ways: listening, speaking, and writing. Compassion is essential. What this distillation overlooks is what makes Thich Nhat Hanh revered: practice. He considers himself to be on a spiritual journey. His journey, however, is not a solo exploration; it seeks to bring all of us along with him. In this sense, his practice of Buddhism, the engagement, is active. And therefore Thich Nhat Hanh is a valuable teacher for us. His lessons serve as inspiration.

While Thich Nhat Hanh is a deeply spiritual man (it is said that he can trace his lineage to Buddha himself), he is deeply aware of the world around him. And while he lives in a monastic community in France, Plum Village, he travels to the United

States frequently and is wholly engaged in our world. He blends his contemplative way of life with a commitment to activism. It was precisely his activism that got him expelled from his homeland.

In interviews with Western media, he comes across as sincere and direct. Those who listen to him come away with a renewed sense of purpose, feeling more in touch with themselves and with others around them. He projects what he preaches: mindfulness and compassion. As he says, "Mindfulness is the capacity to live deeply in the moments of your entire life." With mindfulness, you are living in the moment, and from that springs "freedom from worries, anger and forgetfulness."[48] He believes that "compassion is born from happiness and understanding. When compassion and understanding are kept alive, you are safe."[49] Compassion can be a methodology used in listening to alternative points of view.

## PRACTICAL ADVICE

Meditation is important to Thich Nhat Hanh. He writes in *Creating True Peace* that he and fellow monks participating in Engaged Buddhism had to take at least one day out from helping others in the war zone to renew themselves and their spirits. They did this by participating in a Day of Mindfulness.[50] For those of us in the West, meditation can take place throughout the day—when preparing meals, when driving, or even when answering the phone. "Don't answer it right away; smile and practice one breath in and one breath out to calm yourself," says Thich Nhat Hanh. He applies the same methodology to walking. "Going from one building to another, you can apply mindful walking."[51] Eating, walking, and breathing are life's simplest actions, but for Buddhists in pursuit of connectivity of body, mind, and spirit, they become pathways, or doorways, to self-perfection. For Thich Nhat Hanh, these simple actions are deeply connected to his beliefs.

Children hold a special charm for Thich Nhat Hanh. Perhaps it is because he has a childlike openness about him that he relates to them so well. It is important "to create a living environment where we can feel safe, where our children will feel safe." For Thich Nhat Hanh "a safe environment means a place where the seeds of anger and fear and despair and violence will not be watered everyday. Instead, the seeds of compassion, the seeds of goodness, the seeds of hope will be watered everyday."[52] A child raised without violence and with a respect for mindfulness will become, according to Thich Nhat Hanh, an adult attuned to compassion and peace.

Language is precious to Thich Nhat Hanh. He mixes the language of the earth (seeds, water, flowers) with the language of peace (compassion, understanding, mindfulness, peace). He tells a story in *Anger* about how an "American Buddhist scholar" visiting him in Plum Village and seeing him tend his garden urged him to give up the soil to focus on writing. To which he replied, "My dear friend, if I did not grow lettuce, I could not write the poems I write." As he counsels others to be mindful, he practices it himself. "[I]f you don't live every moment of your daily life deeply, then you cannot write. You can't produce anything valuable to others."[53]

As an author and poet, Thich Nhat Hanh values communication highly. He writes a great deal about the power of listening that involves mindfulness and compassion. By listening mindfully, we can come to understand others better. Dialogue can emerge from such understanding, especially if a relationship has been ruptured. "Train yourself so that you can become skillful enough to restore communication."[54] He also urges us to write letters to others as a means of capturing what is really in our hearts. "In a letter you can be perfectly honest."[55] He also urges us to take our time, even weeks, if necessary. By articulating the steps in communication, both listening and writing, Thich Nhat Hanh provides a methodology for putting mindfulness into practice.

## PURSUIT OF PEACE

Thich Nhat Hanh reminds us over and over again that "Buddha is not a God. Buddha is a human being. He has suffered as a human being."[56] Buddha endured multiple temptations but adhered to the single way of enlightenment.[57] For Thich Nhat Hanh, who has a profound understanding of and respect for Christianity, Buddha's humanity makes him accessible, as Christ's humanity does for Christians. And like some Christians, and unlike many Buddhists, Thich Nhat Hanh's faith propels him to action. For example, he led a peace march against nuclear weapons in New York City in 1982. As he describes it, his small group slowed the pace of some 300,000 peace marchers because as other marchers grew closer to his group, a sense of calm, even mindfulness, came over them. Such is the power of Thich Nhat Hanh's example; even people in a hurry cannot help but be taken by his spirit. For Thich Nhat Hanh, this is not a personal reflection of his supposed powers. He is a profoundly humble man who regards himself merely as a member of the *sangha*, or spiritual community, that has been in motion for more than 2,600 years.[58]

Peace among brothers and peace among nations is an avowed passion for Thich Nhat Hanh. He writes in *Creating True Peace*, "The secret of creating peace is that when you listen to another person you have only one purpose: to offer him an opportunity to empty his heart." He urges world leaders to put this method into practice. If it works between people, why not between nations? This is the way to achieve "true reconciliation." After dissipating "bitterness, fear, and prejudice, people can begin to communicate with each other. Then, reaching peace will be much easier. Peace will become a reality."[59] Coming from a man who has known the devastating impact of war—villages ripped apart, cities bombed, and men, women, and children dying—his words resonate with conviction. For him, can there be any other way but peace? And it starts with individuals, "who must learn how to bring the level of hatred and anger down in themselves and their families so they can support our political leaders, who must do the same thing. Then, when we have enough compassion, we can help the other group of people we might have called enemies to do the same."[60]

The lessons of Thich Nhat Hanh are plentiful. His writings are rich in story and insight. He does not preach so much as instruct, always with a deep understanding of the human condition and wrapped in genuine concern. A man of peace, Thich Nhat Hanh is also a man of love. He sees love as a means of overcoming the destructive forces in our world and in our nature to make us more fully aware. As such, he is an authentic motivator; he creates ways for us to create conditions that allow us to motivate ourselves to live more holistically and in peace.

## Lessons in Leadership Motivation

- *Keep the faith*. Thich Nhat Hanh created a movement called Engaged Buddhism, a form of activism that uses his faith to meet people's social and humanitarian needs.
- *Communicate clearly*. Thich Nhat Hanh is an eloquent writer and poet who expresses himself in the tradition of *dharma*, i.e., providing insight into what might be.
- *Keep it simple and practical*. Thich Nhat Hanh focuses on the smallest details, such as breathing, walking, and eating, as a way of giving people a practical means of attaining mindfulness and compassion.
- *Tell stories*. Thich Nhat Hanh weaves anecdotes and parables into his writing in order to make it authentic and memorable.
- *Live the vision*. Thich Nhat Hanh is a man of peace. He practices his commitment to peace by being mindful of the details and compassionate toward the world.

C H A P T E R

"Successful working relationships are an essential component of our health and success as a business."

*Zingerman's*
*Guiding Principle No. 6*

# CHALLENGE

## OVERCOMING THE ODDS

*I*T WASN'T SOMETHING THAT HE WAS USED TO DOING. *He was a Heisman Trophy winner, after all. But after seven years in the league, the trophy was a part of his résumé that had been forgotten by many. The best collegiate quarterback of 1970 had not blossomed into the best professional quarterback of the subsequent decade. So when the Oakland Raiders asked him to try out for their team, it was a monumental blow to his ego. He was Jim Plunkett. He made the team, but the news was not much better: He* would be the number three quarterback and was not likely to play. From collegiate hero to bench rider—that was a journey.

But Jim Plunkett was not someone who gave up easily. He had learned that from his parents, both of whom were legally blind. His father worked at jobs provided by the state, such as running a news and candy stand, but money was tight, and the family moved frequently. Young Jim was a gifted athlete, with letters in five sports in high school. He was showered with collegiate scholarship offers, but he chose to stay close to home, at Stanford. The Farm was only 10 miles from his parent's home, but culturally it might have been a thousand. The student body then was rich and Waspy; Jim was poor and Hispanic. Sports was his entrée, but he didn't get a chance to distinguish himself immediately; he was diagnosed with a tumor in upper torso. The good news was that the tumor was not malignant; the bad news was that recuperation from surgery prevented him from playing freshman football.

Jim recovered, but the coach suggested that he move to defense. Plunkett refused; he liked Stanford, but he loved being a quarterback. By his junior year he had turned doubters into believers, and in his senior year he led his team to the Rose Bowl and beat a highly touted Ohio State team.

With Heisman in hand, his move to the NFL was logical, but his progress was not magical. He was a number one draft choice for the New England Patriots and won Rookie of the Year honors in 1971. He played in every game until injuries sidelined him in 1975 and he was traded to San Francisco. When the offer to try out for the Raiders came in 1978, Jim was on the verge of giving up the game. Instead, he put aside his pride and accepted. After not playing at all in 1978 and only occasionally in 1979, Jim wanted out of Oakland. Then, five weeks into the 1980 season, the starting quarterback, Dan Pastorini, a rival of Jim's since boyhood, broke his leg. Jim stepped in and led the Raiders, a team noted as much for misfits as for prowess, to a string of victories. And in 1981 he took them to the Super Bowl, where they trounced the Philadelphia Eagles. Jim was named Super Bowl MVP. The next year two years were not so super, but in 1983, after the team had moved to Los Angeles, Plunkett *again led the Raiders to the promised land—another Super Bowl title in 1984.*

*Although football is essentially a team game, those who stand apart are treated like heroes. Jim Plunkett, unlike some quarterbacks of his era, was an exception. He was a team-first guy; his natural ability as a thrower contributed to his ability to bring a team together—not an easy task with a team like the Raiders. He made overcoming adversity part of his nature. His resiliency was perhaps his greatest strength. Al Davis, the principal owner of the Raiders and a man known to be parsimonious with praise, says of his former quarterback, "He has to be one of the great comeback stories of our time." A man of few words, Jim Plunkett led as he motivated, by example.[1]*

✍ ✍

Nothing fuels the human spirit so much as a challenge. Whether it is an athlete like Jim Plunkett seeking to overcome the odds or a CEO trying to reinvigorate his company, nothing motivates people more than having a goal. For individuals, goals emerge from inside; they are formed around what makes us happy, which may be recognition of our efforts, increased financial rewards, or the inner glow that results when we do a good turn for someone. For organizations, goals emerge from a combination of circumstances and leadership. The circumstances are the situation in which the organization operates; they are shaped by market, social, and competitive factors. The leaders of an organization size up the organization and decide where it must go and how it must get there. But leaders do not do this by themselves; they do it with the collective energy of the people in the organization.

## MAKE THE CHALLENGE CLEAR

A good example of issuing a challenge and following up can be found in the example of A.G. Lafley, CEO of Procter & Gamble. Lafley inherited a company that had lost its spark. His predecessor had believed that he could cost-cut his way to improved financial performance. All companies cut, but few do it well, and P&G was no exception. In contrast to his predecessor, Lafley sought to leverage the power of P&G's people and challenge them to grow the company creatively. His formula, coupled with some key acquisitions, worked. From 2000 through 2004, P&G's earnings increased, not just through acquisitions, but from existing business units. According to *Fortune* magazine, what Lafley did is what many successful executives do: focus on the customer, reinvigorate the brands, and promote innovation. But he did something more; he communicated simply and directly to his team. While *Fortune* editor Patricia Sellers teased Lafley about his use of clichés, he took it in stride and reminded her, "There is a lot of jargon. But we have to find things that are simple for 100,000 people to understand. And more than half of my organization doesn't have English as a first language. So it's intentional."[2] When you keep things simple, but not simple-minded, you can ensure that the mission remains clear, coherent, and compelling. In other words, what Lafley did was make the challenge real and tangible for everyone in the organization.

- *Identify opportunities.* Every child is asked, "What do you want to be when you grow up?" Leaders of organizations need to ask themselves the very same question. Entrepreneurs excel at answering this question because it is the question that gives rise to their business. For example, Fred Smith thought it would be possible to create a direct-shipping network that could offer next-day delivery. Michael Dell wondered how he might apply the direct-selling model to personal computers. Jeff Bezos conceived the possibility of a global online bookstore. Such thinking spawned Federal Express, Dell Computer, and Amazon.com, respectively, but such thinking has also enabled others, like A.G. Lafley of P&G, to rethink their business models. Carlos Gutierrez at Kellogg Company has recast the venerable cereal maker as a provider of breakfast foods, while Jeffrey Immelt at General Electric has pushed his company to become much more entrepreneurial. None of these leaders did solo acts. They discovered opportunities and made others enthusiastic about following their lead.

- *Frame the challenge.* Once an opportunity has been selected, the leader needs to bring others into the act. She must frame the organizational challenge as an opportunity for personal growth. One of the best ways to motivate people is to give them a challenge. This challenge may take the form of a new project, such as developing a new marketing plan, or it may be a process of discovering new ways of doing things. Some organizations call these "stretch goals," meaning that they expand an individual's capability. At pharmaceutical companies, challenges are a way of life—discovering new compounds to use for next-generation drugs. It is a high-risk, high-reward enterprise, but it fosters a strong culture of creativity and innovation. In short, people are motivated to succeed because the conditions around them foster their own innate desire to achieve. Managers who seek the right challenges for their people and support those challenges with the right blend of delegation and support will achieve good success.

- *Make the challenge real but attainable.* Every challenge needs to reach for the sky; otherwise it will fail to capture the imagination of those who can make it happen. Ari Weinzweig and Paul Saginaw of Zingerman's have found a terrific way to make entrepreneurial dreams come true for their employees: giving them a stake in new business opportunities. That is how the company expanded from a delicatessen into other food-related businesses. They turned the challenge of keeping good people into a business opportunity and supported those people along the way. By contrast, if the challenge is too far out there, instead of inspiring people, you will only frustrate them.

## THE CREATIVE ORGANIZATION

Identifying, framing, and supporting challenges is in essence a balancing act, but one way to keep people focused is to engage their creative spirit. Creativity complements the challenge. All too often we tend to think of creativity as something that is reserved for college students who don't have a clue about what to do or artists who hover in a zone between reality and fantasy. That misconception is costly. The human condition has evolved because of people's perpetual striving for new, different, and better ways of doing things. If this were not the case, our toolbox would consist of nothing more than a single hammer. Or, in the IT world, development would have stopped with ENIAC. (Try bringing that behemoth along on your next flight.) Creativity is the pursuit of ideas. It spurs innovation, which you may consider as the transformation of an idea into an action, e.g., moving from electronic scanning to television, from voice over wire to telephony, or from the Internet to e-commerce. Managers play an essential role in stimulating creativity. Here are some ways to use communications to encourage creativity.

- *Think differently.* Great ideas begin with thinking. Our corporate culture militates against thinking because we are evaluated on our output, with emphasis on the *out*. Thinking is given a low priority because we tend not to value it. Managers can encourage others to take the time to think by doing it themselves and talking about it. Not everything we conceive of should be attempted, but when one idea is combined with two, three, or four others, the result might turn out to be a breakthrough. Make a habit of talking about ideas.

- *Feed the mind.* Athletes prepare their bodies for competition through exercise and proper diet. You need to prepare your mind to think by feeding it with information designed to trigger thought. Managers can prepare the minds of their folks to think by developing an energy room for a special project. Inside it you can post images and articles related to the project on the walls. You can do the same with a bulletin board, or even on a Web site. The purpose of the room is to stimulate thought. (*Hint:* Brainstorming sessions can be "nurtured" by the addition of snacks, fruit, and beverages—food for the body, too.)

* *Stage creative off-sites.* For many people, off-sites are an opportunity to focus on issues and formulate solutions. Off-sites can also serve another purpose: an ideation session. The point here is to prepare people in advance and then structure activities designed to stimulate thought. It's a good idea to hire a professional facilitator or creativity consultant to help with these sessions, but if you must do it yourself, look for indirect ways to stimulate thought. Consider ruminative thinking, where people have an opportunity to think about an issue or problem in advance. Through brainstorming and creativity sessions focusing on narratives or pictograms, you can stimulate good thoughts and some creative ideas that you can channel into solutions, processes, or products. Do not always swing for the fences at these off-sites; what you are looking for are ideas or germs of ideas that can lead to bigger ideas or projects. If you come up with the next-generation product, wonderful, but don't expect this.

There is an innate desire to succeed in all of us. It falls to the leader to unlock that desire and channel it to the organization's best purpose. In doing so, she weaves the individual's need for success with the organization's need to achieve results for its customers and constituents. When challenges are issued and then managed and supported with concern and creativity, much can be accomplished. The conditions for motivation flourish, and people and organizations flourish.

## Insights into Motivation: Dale Carnegie

The essence of motivation is winning the confidence of others. To do that, you need to understand people and be able to present well. Those are two attributes that define Dale Carnegie. A salesperson turned public speaker, Dale Carnegie has influenced generations of men and women, and along the way legitimized the self-help industry. His insights are common sense, but they are presented in an "uncommonly sensible" way, so that his lessons are accessible and understandable. As business author Stuart Cranier writes, "Carnegie's message remains relevant: people matter and, in the world of business, how you manage and relate to people is the key to success."[3] Carnegie's masterpiece, *How to Win Friends and Influence People*, published in 1936, has sold more than 10 million copies. That's quite a motivational fact in itself. Strategy guru and best-selling author Gary Hamel summed up Carnegie this way: "Though Dale Carnegie's advice borders on the manipulative, it is warm and fuzzy, eager salesman kind of manipulation." In other words, you buy what he's selling—the virtues of self-improvement.[4]

## Motivation Planner: Challenge

People respond to a challenge because it taps their inner desire to succeed. What leaders need to do is frame the challenge as accessible and attainable. Use the following questions to see how you can create challenges for your people.

Creating a challenge requires creativity and commitment. Consider the following.

1. What are the issues your organization is facing? How can you break those challenges down into action steps that will ignite the imagination of your people?
2. How can you frame the challenges as opportunities? That is, what can you do to make what needs doing exciting and energizing for your people?
3. How can you make the challenges in your organization accessible to your people? Aim too high, and you will burn people out. Aim too low, and you will bore people. Find the right balance.
4. How can you support the people on your team so that they can achieve the challenges? Be careful not to micro-manage.
5. How will you encourage your direct reports to create challenges for their people?

## ZINGERMAN'S: ARI WEINZWEIG AND PAUL SAGINAW

When you see the place for the first time, with its windows crammed with foodstuffs and imported cheeses, salamis, and hams, it may remind you of the food stores you've seen in historical photographs of urban immigrant America at the turn of the twentieth century. Upon a closer look, you notice the handmade posters featuring the zany graphics that are a hallmark of the store. You have arrived at Zingerman's, one of the most famous delicatessens in the nation. *Food & Wine* magazine selected Zingerman's as one of the top 25 food stores in the entire world, and one of only two in the United States.[5] And *Inc.* magazine called it the "coolest small company in America."[6] The selection of foods is mind-boggling: directly imported farmhouse cheeses, cured meats, smoked fish, complemented by bread from Zingerman's own bakery, which it uses for more than 50 different kinds of sandwiches. But what distinguishes this store, located in Ann Arbor, Michigan, is something that most patrons recognize but never really consider: the attention to detail that ensures that what is offered is the best of the best in everything from olive oil to balsamic vinegar to caviar and homemade gelato. Each of these foods has its origins as an authentic peasant food. (Yes, once upon a time caviar was a salty fish byproduct offered free to sailors in port to encourage them to drink more.[7])

## AUTHENTIC MANAGEMENT

Authenticity is the hallmark of Zingerman's and the watchword of its two principal owners, Ari Weinzweig and Paul Saginaw. While Zingerman's itself is an homage to the palate, it is rooted in and nurtured by a culture that is people-centric. In fact, word of Zingerman's remarkable commitment to customer service and training has gotten out beyond the food community, with the result that demand for its consulting and training services is growing. Health-care providers, financial institutions, and high-tech businesses are eager customers, as are many other businesses that serve consumers directly. As a measure of that success, ZingTrain, the business that sprang from the company's need for internal training but now spends most of its time providing training for companies, was recognized by *T&D*, a leading publication in the training and development field, as an outstanding resource. The reason for Zingerman's remarkable success in both food and training is no secret: It's a commitment to its people that starts the moment a person is hired.

Founded in 1982, Zingerman's is not simply a deli; it's a community of businesses that besides the deli includes a bakery, a catering service, a mail-order house, and a training business. Total revenues approach $25 million annually. The distinguishing factor in this community is that the managing partners of these businesses have an equity stake in the enterprise. It really *is* their business, and they treat it accordingly. This is why customers are amazed by the attentive service, the knowledgeable and patient staff, and that staff's sheer enthusiasm for good food and good service. Zingerman's employees take pride in what they do, and it shows.

## FROM VALUE TO OPERATIONS

Zingerman's commitment to its people is reflected in its eight guiding principles. There are guidelines for food, service, and profits, but the remaining principles are focused on people. Take Guiding Principle No. 5: A Great Place to Work! Empowerment resonates in the opening statement: "Working at Zingerman's means taking an active part in running the business." Underscoring this principle are discussions of creativity, compensation, growth, development, safety, diversity, and, of course, fun.[8] Subsequent principles underscore the need for building relationships with customers and among staff, including recognition of individual and group successes.[9] As partner Paul Saginaw says, "I think that people want to be part of something that is much greater than themselves. . . . My job is to turn those held values into operational values. I think that's one area where we differ from other organizations."[10]

Such values are "promises." As Saginaw explains, "And if I keep that promise, they trust me. What greater asset can a leader or an employer have than the trust of the people who are going to follow?" Saginaw puts the onus on the leadership: "And if I don't keep that promise, and I lose that trust, then as an organization, then I don't believe we'll be able to accomplish much at all." Citing management philosopher Peter Drucker, Saginaw says, "People who work with you give you a gift, the gift of followership. And in return you owe them a debt. Part of that debt is to provide an environment where they feel safe enough to bring their best efforts."[11]

## LEADING BY EXAMPLE

Leaders must show the way. "You always should be aware that you are being watched," says Saginaw. "People are making opinions based on what you do. It's very important to come to work and be upbeat and to spread goodwill and sunshine throughout your organization. Leading by example is paramount. I think it's the only way people learn." Example begins with little things, especially in the food trade. Says Saginaw, "It is picking up the mop, picking up the paper, opening the door. . . . It's doing all the things that they don't expect you to do. And doing them all the time!" Setting the right example extends to the shop floor. "My focus and my time is always going to go to the least-empowered person in the room," says Saginaw, adding, "because they need me the most." There is another reason to reach out—to teach other managers. "[T]he person who has the least authority and the least power is the most important person for you to put your time into."[12] Zingerman's as an institution demonstrates its commitment to the welfare of its employees by offering health and employee assistance benefits to all full-time employees who have passed their orientation training programs, something that can happen in as little as 60 days.

Learning is also a core principle, with the focus being on education about food, the business, and job tasks. At Zingerman's, nothing is taken for granted. This learning begins with an orientation process that Weinzweig himself leads. During a two-hour session, he focuses on the company's mission and guiding principles, with special emphasis on how its vision, supported by its principles, culture, and systems, delivers results or, as Zingerman's says, "great food, great service, great finance." Most of the new front-line employees are very young, in their late teens and early twenties. For them, Zingerman's probably will not be a career, but you would not know that from watching Ari in action. As many times as he has delivered this presentation, which is highly interactive, his eyes still twinkle. He is genuinely excited about what he does, and it rubs off on the employees. Weinzweig passes out food samples and invites the employees to inspect, smell, and taste them. Through this exercise, he explores the origins of artisanal food and talks about the Zingerman's mission to make food the old-fashioned way. And this is a world expert, with years of exploring, cooking, presenting, and writing about food to his credit. Weinzweig does not talk down to his audience; he engages their imagination, and they drink in his message enthusiastically. And by the end of the session he has them using the first-person pronoun: *our* food, *our* service, *our* finance, and *our* business.

Enthusiasm will only go so far in the food business. There are many people who are passionate about food, but still, as Saginaw and Weinzweig will attest, go out of business in a hurry. Currently, as part of its commitment to open-book management, Zingerman's is pushing the financial education of its employees. This starts at orientation. Weinzweig talks about the need for accuracy and tells a tale of a missing brownie, that is, one that was not given to someone who ordered it. Spinning the yarn, he tells the new hires that the person who ordered it lives in Toledo, some fifty miles away. Of course, Zingerman's will drive the brownie to the customer, a trip, including the cost of the brownie, that might run as high as $50. The employees nod affirmatively; they had never imagined that one lost brownie could be so expensive.

But the lesson is not over. Assuming a 5 percent return, which is standard in food service, the cost of that missing brownie must be paid for out of profits, not gross revenue. As a result, to break even on the brownie, the deli must sell $1,000 worth of food. *That* number grabs the employees' attention. Slowly, as Ari coaches them, the new hires come to realize that accuracy is not something that's nice to do; it's an imperative. This lesson is one small way in which Zingerman's develops the entrepreneurial mindset; employees are eligible for incentives and bonuses, but such rewards can be given only when the company turns a profit. Hence the brownie story becomes not just a good story, but the beginning of an education in fiscal responsibility.

Lessons in finance are repeated many times during the day and hundreds of thousands of times throughout the course of the year. The way to make open-book management work is to make it truly *open*. Financial statements are a means of keeping score, but at Zingerman's the score is tallied right on the front lines—and out in the open—in what the company calls "huddles." As

Weinzweig describes them, "the huddles are really the place from which the operations of the business are run. In under an hour at a business's huddle I have a great sense of what's going on," in food, finance, and service.[13] The focus of the huddles is the department's operating reports, which track between "5 and 25 different line items," including operation measurements but also "check average, on-time deliveries, and mystery-shopping ratings." The devil may be in the details, but details such as these may be the difference between a loss and a profit, especially in low-margin operations such as food service.[14]

Huddles also provide an insight into people management issues, specifically, "who on the staff is actively participating, who's on their game, who understands what we're doing, who's a bit disengaged and may need some extra attention, [and] who the up-and-coming leaders are."[15] All of this takes time and effort. Managing people the right way in a culture that affirms their dignity is not easy. It is a time-intensive task that is not only mentally challenging but also physically draining. What's more, motivating employees who have tuned out is a challenge for any organization, but these employees are also a resource, especially after they have been trained. How to reach them? Weinzweig uses dialogue. "It might end up that they don't want to be there, but you won't know unless you reach out to them." As he says, "If you don't reach out to them, what happens? It just gets worse."[16]

## LEVERAGING THE LESSONS

Getting people to believe in themselves is another way leaders motivate. "You don't want to ask people to do anything that you wouldn't do. [Also,] you don't require people to do things that they currently aren't capable of doing. And if you want them to move further than that, you push their horizons gently. . . . [T]hen you will be able to get people to reach beyond their self-imposed limitations and start to accomplish things they didn't think possible."[17]

Failure is a powerful teacher and motivator, explains Saginaw. "I think you can reward people for failure, for the attempt."

As he says laughingly, "If you want to teach a bear to dance, you gotta reward the wiggle." Becoming more serious, Saginaw says, "And so I think it's important to allow people to move along by giving them projects that are somewhat lower risk where you can allow them to fail and then sit down and say, 'Okay, what did we learn?'" That is a powerful lesson for people: realizing that a mistake will not cost them their job.[18]

Teaching managers to manage is a continual challenge. Typically, most managers believe that they must be experts and problem solvers. Saginaw turns the tables by explaining that managers are enablers, getting others to be the experts and the problem solvers. As Saginaw explains, "The organization is going to move forward not by you [the manager] becoming smarter, it's by taking the lowest-performing person on your staff and raising the level of their performance up. We raise up from the bottom, we don't pull it up from the top." As he tells his new managers, "[T]he health, the growth, the well-being, the development of your staff . . . is your ultimate charge. They are the ones that are going to be taking care of all the customers."[19]

Coaching continues for managers. Saginaw may spend time reviewing performance reviews and notice an overly critical trend. He will say to the manager, "You seem to be showing that they are doing a lot of things wrong. Are they doing anything right? Can we lead with appreciation here?" Such questions will provoke a dialogue and begin to orient the manager toward learning to manage with more affirmation. Zingerman's is not a place for slackers, however; those who do not respond to coaching or, worse, fail to uphold the values of the organization are asked to leave. As Saginaw explains, "Morale and performance drive the culture, not vice versa." As he also states, "Change the performance level [for the better]. And then you'll change the culture."[20]

## LOOKING AHEAD

One reason for Zingerman's success is its focus on the future. Most food businesses, because they offer what is fresh, hot, and now (both figuratively and literally), live in the here and now. They cannot look too far ahead. Zingerman's, by contrast, as a community of businesses, is looking ahead. It has been creating, and following, five-year plans for some time. In fact, it was this sense of planning ahead that led to the shared enterprise concept. And, of course, having a vision statement, a mission statement, and guiding principles that are freely available to employees communicates the sincerity of the endeavor. Weinzweig and Saginaw are committed to following what they have created.

The process that led to the vision statement was born out of middle-aged angst—where did the partners want their decade-old business to go? Weinzweig credits Saginaw with pushing the envelope. "He's just good at asking out-of-the-box questions that often go unasked." Saginaw wondered if they shouldn't open Zingerman's delis in other cities; Weinzweig was against it. "There were lots of disagreements during that year, but there've been lots before that and lots since." What holds the partners together is another form of agreement. Explains Weinzweig, "If we can't come to agreement, we don't act, and . . . we'll keep coming back to the table till we do. . . . The key is that we share a commitment to the same vision and the same values."[21]

The vision, "2009: A Food Odyssey," written in the form of a letter by Ari, begins poetically with the image of the trademark black bench that has been in front of the deli since its doors were first opened for business. Playing with the concept of the bench as a benchmark (get it?), Weinzweig weaves the tale of how he and Paul used the bench as a meeting place to plot the next chapters in the Zingerman's story. As Ari tells it, their discussions focused not on franchising but on growing the business through multiple extensions, e.g., a coffee shop, bakery, creamery, and mail-order house for starters; there might eventually be as many as a dozen or more businesses in the Zingerman's community. As Ari writes, "[Our] commitment is to work with each of our new partners to share our experience, our systems, our ideas, our insights, our help, in working to help make these new businesses effective parts of the Zingerman's family." And Ari and Paul know when to take a back seat, or, as Ari puts it, "a benchseat," when it comes to managing the community businesses—something that is not typical of entrepreneurs. The spotlight belongs on the managing partners; it's their show to run.[22] These words, backed by Weinzweig and Saginaw's example, are powerful motivators for people who want to develop their entrepreneurial talents. Very importantly, Weinzweig and Saginaw want to keep their business in Ann Arbor. It is a community that they cherish and help to nurture with their businesses as well as their personal commitment.

## GIVING BACK

Weinzweig and Saginaw put their values (as stipulated by Guiding Principle No. 8) to work in the community. In 1985, Zingerman's helped establish Food Gatherers, a service distributing perishable food to those in need; the organization distributes some one million pounds annually. Zingerman's is also active in other community service events and actively encourages its employees to participate. "I believe you earn the right to compete in the competitive marketplace in your community," says Saginaw. Earning that right involves "choosing a site responsibly, building responsibly, hiring responsibly, making a profit responsibly, and sharing that profit responsibly with the people in your organization and the community."[23]

Zingerman's has become an icon of American food. While its variety of artisanal foods will continue to grow as demand for the new and different, as well as the tried and true, escalates, the lasting legacy of Zingerman's may be the generations of workers it has educated as employees or training patrons. Its lessons about how to treat people right in ways that enrich the psyche as well as improve the bottom line may be the most valuable of all. And it is for that reason that Zingerman's stands out as a place where motivation flourishes because the conditions are rich and ripe for people to accomplish their goals, thanks to the ongoing commitment that Ari Weinzweig and Paul Saginaw have made to their people.

## Lessons in Leadership Motivation

- *Articulate the values.* Zingerman's has a mission statement and guiding principles that it teaches and reinforces in training and in daily practice.
- *Open the books.* Ari Weinzweig and Paul Saginaw employ open-book management. Employees know what things cost, what they earn, and how much the business profits. Knowing the balance sheet fosters responsibility and a sense of ownership.
- *"Taste the food."* At Zingerman's, food is the business; employees are taught to smell, taste, and appreciate it, and to teach what they know. Metaphorically speaking, tasting the food can apply to experiencing the business from the inside out.
- *Teach always.* Ari Weinzweig and Paul Saginaw are relentless teachers. Each focuses on his respective competencies, but both teach the principles of business and people management to their managers and employees.
- *Turn "your" into "our."* Zingerman's emphasizes collective responsibility. Serving customers with great food is not what *they* do, it's what *we* do. The use of *our* connotes ownership of issues, problems, and opportunities.
- *Provide incentives for what you want to get done.* Zingerman's offers cash rewards to employees who become certified in their core skills prior to posted deadlines. This encourages people to qualify early, which makes them more valuable employees.
- *Make the future real.* Ari Weinzweig and Paul Saginaw grow businesses as they grow people: with an

eye to the future, which they find "energizing" and
"exciting," not to mention highly motivating to their
people and themselves.[24]

- *Live the example.* Ari Weinzweig and Paul Saginaw
  have created a community of food-related businesses
  that operates on the principles of treating people
  fairly, equitably, and with a stake in the enterprise.

# Encourage

- *Empower*
- *Coach*
- *Recognize*

*M*otivation demands encouragement. Leadership is a journey, a process of moving from one place to another. Sometimes it is easy; most often it is hard and demanding. Leaders must therefore encourage their people along the way. They can do this by empowering their people, coaching them to excellence, and recognizing their achievements. Encouragement breeds motivation.

C H A P T E R

"Partnership involves money—which is crucial to
any business relationship—but it also involves basic
human considerations, such as respect."

*Sam Walton*
*Founder, Wal-Mart*

"You're the only one who can make the difference.
Whatever your dream is, go for it."

*Earvin "Magic" Johnson*
*Entrepreneur/Philanthropist*

# EMPOWER

## SELF-EMPOWERMENT

*F*OR A MAN OF SUCH AFFIRMATION, *it is amazing how many
people have told him no. From the police who beat him
senseless on the Edmund Pettus Bridge in Selma, Alabama, in 1965 to the party bosses in Atlanta who didn't want him*

running against Julian Bond, John Lewis has refused to take no for an answer when he believed he was in the right.

The son of a sharecropper, Lewis was a shy, awkward boy who felt more at home talking to chickens than to people. Even his family thought him a bit odd, too much of a loner. He sought a way out and found it through education, and also through social protest. As a young Freedom Rider, he was arrested and jailed more than forty times, once for a month in Mississippi's infamous Parchman Farm.

Even the president told Lewis no. In 1963, as the leader of the Student Non-Violent Coordinating Committee, he and five other leaders from the civil rights movement met with John F. Kennedy, who asked them to call off the scheduled March on Washington. Kennedy feared a backlash that would cripple him politically and damage the movement. The leaders refused, and the march went on; it proved to be a galvanizing moment in the struggle for freedom and dignity. Lewis's own speech at the Lincoln Memorial was heavily edited by the elders of the movement, who asked Lewis to remove all criticisms of the president, something that as a young student leader he found demeaning, but now, with the hindsight of history, finds appropriate.

The nos that Lewis heard throughout his formative years and even into adulthood did not wear down his spirit. After being voted out of the leadership of SNCC in favor of those who were more radical, like Stokely Carmichael, Lewis went to New York City and found work writing grants for social service agencies. He married and went back to the South, to Atlanta. He lost a bid for the city council, but a decade later he decided to run for Congress against the formidable and telegenic Julian Bond. To the surprise of everyone except himself, Lewis won. ("People had always underestimated me," he once said.)

He took his crusade for justice and equal rights to Congress, but he had no knee-jerk response to all African-American issues. He opposed the nomination of Clarence Thomas because of Thomas's stance against affirmative action, of which he (Thomas) had been the beneficiary. He drew the ire of the Black

*Congressional Caucus because he opposed its organization and support by the Nation of Islam, which Lewis considered anti-Semitic.*

*For Lewis, justice must indeed be color-blind. This is the only way in which people will be able to help themselves to the good things that society has to offer. On an equal playing field, people can empower themselves. The driving force within empowerment is faith in one's self and faith in others. This requires courage, something that John Lewis embodies and addressed in his acceptance speech for the John F. Kennedy Profile in Courage award for 2001. "Courage is a reflection of the heart—it is a reflection of something deep within the man or woman or even a child who must resist and must defy an authority that is morally wrong. Courage makes us march on despite fear and doubt on the road toward justice."[1]*

⋞⋙ ⋞⋙

Seldom do the words "march to the beat of your own drummer" apply to a member of the U.S. Senate, which sharply marshals and divides its members according to party affiliation. Daniel Patrick Moynihan was a notable exception. A Harvard professor, ambassador to the United Nations, social policy analyst, four-term U.S. senator, and author or coauthor of 19 books, Moynihan mixed with people of all political stripes. He served four presidents, Kennedy, Johnson, Nixon, and Ford—two Democrats and two Republicans. His ability to get along with those with whom his party disagreed was a result of the centrality of his cause: the poor and the disadvantaged.

Having endured a degree of poverty while growing up, he knew what it was like to go without; his family had been abandoned by his father when he was a boy. After a year of college, he enlisted in the Navy during World War II and entered an officer's training corps program. After the war, he tended a bar his mother owned in Hell's Kitchen during the summers when he was home from college. He won a Fulbright scholarship to the London

*School of Economics. There he lived the life of a bon vivant for a while, all the while working and writing his Ph.D. dissertation. (He never lost his taste for the good life. His wife, Eileen, said that she married him because he was the funniest person she had ever met, his Ph.D. index card files contained a large number of recipes for mixed drinks, and he offered visitors to his Senate office a glass of dry sherry.)*

*After earning his Ph.D., he moved to Washington with his family and entered the Kennedy administration, working in the Department of Labor and rising to assistant secretary. On the day Kennedy was shot, Moynihan urged anyone in government who would listen to put Lee Harvey Oswald into protective custody as the first step in the investigation into the assassination. His words about Oswald were not heeded, but his television interview, given on the Sunday after the assassination, was. He said about Kennedy: "I don't think there's any point in being Irish if you don't know that the world is going to break your heart eventually. I guess we thought he had a little more time." He then added sotto voce, "So did he."*

*A gifted and learned communicator both in print and aloud, Moynihan, as the* New York Times *said in his obituary, "was less an original researcher than a bold, often brilliant synthesizer whose works compelled furious debate and further research." It was his ability to synthesize, taking good ideas from wherever they emerged, that was the secret of his intellect. He admired the left for its commitment to social uplifting; he took note of the right for its insistence on the primacy of the family as a bulwark against social erosion. As a result, he was both praised and excoriated by both.*

*More a gadfly than a legislator, he was hailed by Edward Kennedy as someone who demonstrated "what the Founding Fathers thought the Senate would be about." He was an artful debater, a good friend to his colleagues, and a faithful quipster to journalists, who mourned his passing in 2003 at the age of 76. Comity for the sake of the disadvantaged was his lifelong mantra. He wrote in 1967 that liberals should "see more clearly*

*that their essential interest is in the stability of the social order"*
*and toward that end should "make alliances with conservatives*
*who share that concern." His seeking of comity amidst chaos*
*enabled both sides to see virtue in his ideas and make the world*
*a better place.*[2]

Empower. This may have been one of the most overused words in
the management lexicon of the eighties and nineties. A story
about the concept illustrates why it has fallen into disrepute. A
major manufacturing company was going through one of its periodic reorganizations. Some consultant had sold it on the concept
of getting its employees more involved in decision-making, and a
firm had been hired to develop an empowerment tool kit to help
managers learn to delegate more effectively. So far so good. Well,
the launch of the tool kit left much to be desired. One manager
had such faith in the process that he called his team together,
tossed the empowerment tool kit on the table, and told them that
he would be back in 45 minutes. Actually, the concept of letting
the team discover the process for itself is a form of empowerment, but since empowerment involves delegation, the fact that
the manager walked away from a process that he was to lead and
thereby demonstrate the validity of empowering others shows
you why the process and the word have gotten a bad rap. However, at the risk of tilting at windmills, I would like to revive the
concept and, more importantly, demonstrate that it is essential to
creating an environment in which motivation can occur.

## DUTY TO DELEGATE

Empowerment begins with self-empowerment. As we have
seen, John Lewis and Daniel P. Moynihan believed that they
could make a difference and took it upon themselves to make
that difference, joining with many hundreds of thousands of

like-minded men and women who believed in the cause of civil rights. Empowerment begins with a belief in yourself and a willingness to give something of yourself so that others can participate in the endeavor, whether it be a social movement or a business enterprise.

When people do not empower themselves, they lack the confidence to empower others. One reason why empowerment has failed to take hold is failure to delegate the authority to do the job. All too often, managers put people in charge of a project but fail to give them the authority to get the job done. For example, a senior executive may ask a manager to work with the marketing department to develop a new launch campaign. However, the executive fails to inform the people in marketing of this and gives the manager no resources or budget to carry out the assignment. The manager is responsible for the project, but does not have the tools needed to succeed. This is akin to hiring a general contractor to build a home, but not giving him the authority to hire carpenters, masonry workers, electricians, and plumbers to assist him. Any assignment where responsibility is dispensed without authority will quickly run into roadblocks. The process will alienate those involved because they will be responsible for the lack of results and will be expecting discipline rather than kudos. Is it any wonder, then, that the concept of empowerment has become so tarnished?

Empowerment is about delegating both responsibility and authority. Sam Walton began his retail business with a single store. There is no way he could have expanded much beyond a couple of stores without delegating both responsibility and authority to others. And as his company, Wal-Mart, grew, he pushed decision-making throughout the company. He wanted his store managers and department managers to think the way he did—like entrepreneurs with a stake in the business. The core of any empowerment effort, as Walton understood, is decision-making. It also affirms the value of employees because the act of granting them responsibility and authority demonstrates that you have faith in them. That is a very powerful motivational concept. Here are some ways to make empowerment a reality in the workplace.

- *Identify opportunities*. Leaders are responsible for grooming their successors. Empowerment is an ideal way to give people real decision-making authority in order to see what they are capable of doing. A leader, therefore, should be looking for job assignments that she can delegate to employees in order to develop their leadership acumen. At Southwest Airlines, leadership roles are offered to employees first; it makes for a stronger culture. Pick an assignment that is doable without heroics. You want to create opportunities for the employee to grow but not to snap. Too much responsibility too soon can burn someone out and discourage him from ever seeking responsibility again. Choose the assignment wisely.

- *Give responsibility.* Once an opportunity has been identified, invite an employee to participate. Give him the option of saying no, but encourage him to say yes. For example, suppose your department needs a team leader for a new project. Identify the employee you want to offer the position to, and have a conversation about it. Discuss the parameters of the project, including the new responsibilities. Make certain you invite questions. If the employee accepts, agree on the scope, resources, budget, and time frame of the project. Make certain you tell the employee that he is in charge, but that you will be available. Insist on regular reports. That's exactly what Sam Walton and his leadership team did.

- *Distribute authority*. Giving the employee the authority to do the job is essential. Responsibility without authority is like an unfunded government mandate. It is something that you have to do, but you have no money or authority to do it. Make certain the employee knows that she is in charge. Also, make certain that her peers know this, too. Again emphasize your availability if she wants your advice. Do not impose it, however, until things go bad. That's a lesson that Southwest Airlines lives. It gives people the freedom to stretch and to grow.

- *Hold people accountable.* Responsibility and authority build character and increase the leadership capability of the individual. But this can happen only if the individual is held accountable for the results. "Success has many fathers," said John F. Kennedy, quoting an old adage, "but failure is an orphan." Kennedy was talking about the failure of the Bay of Pigs invasion in Cuba. While Kennedy assumed responsibility for this fiasco, even though it was hatched on President Eisenhower's watch, he did learn from the experience. Never again would he implicitly trust the military or the CIA, a lesson that served him well 18 months later during the Cuban missile crisis. Failure is a good teacher, albeit a painful one. It is easy to get people to be accountable when things go right; it is harder to get them to face the truth when they have made mistakes.

- *Empower unto others.* One of the benefits of empowering employees is that when it is done well, it spreads throughout the organization. Once managers see their leaders empowering, they follow their example, and this continues until you have pushed decision making to the front lines. Nordstrom is famous for one sentence in its employee handbook: Do what is right for the customer. While times have changed, that statement guides the department store and inspires many other customer-service organizations. Ritz-Carlton walks the empowerment walk with its employee credo that grants front-line people the responsibility to deal with customers honestly and the authority to care for them professionally. Everything in the Ritz-Carlton culture is directed toward fulfilling its brand promise that the customer comes first. This can occur only when employees are provided with the training and management support they need in order to embrace this credo. Wishing for empowerment is not enough; you have to put the systems into place to support it.

## EMPOWERMENT AS LIBERATION

There is a flip side to empowerment: management freedom. Encouraging decision making at the employee level and delegating authority and responsibility to those employees is an act of liberation. As the manager, you will have time to focus on leading the enterprise. This means that you will be working to reinforce the organization's vision, mission, and values. You do this by encouraging the talents of others and putting them into positions of responsibility where they can continue to grow and develop the organization along with you.

You will not be checking out of your job. You will still need to follow up on employee decisions and monitor their progress reports. You also need to be in the loop in order to provide assistance and advice. Being available to help is not micromanagement. Larry Bossidy, former CEO of Allied Signal and Honeywell and coauthor of *Execution,* reminds us that senior leaders owe it to their employees to supervise as long as they do not remove decision-making and responsibility.[3] Senior leaders should be around to provide advice and keep projects on track, especially if those projects start to veer widely from their goals. Sometimes a friendly word of caution or a well-timed question will help the employee discover for herself what needs to be corrected. Such advice not only is good leadership but further encourages the development of a climate for motivation. Earvin "Magic" Johnson is someone who has acted upon what he has learned and created a climate in which motivation can occur. As a basketball player, he listened to his coaches and passed along the lessons to his teammates. As an individual with the HIV virus, he passes along the message of living healthfully. As an entrepreneur, he gained knowledge from Hollywood moguls and invested his money and his learnings wisely to build a vibrant business empire.

The net result of successful empowerment, when people have responsibility and authority, is trust. Leaders trust their people, and people trust their leaders. Mutual trust creates strong bonds that hold the organization together. It makes the organization stronger as well as more efficient. People can speak in shorthand to one another, without going into great detail, because they know one another's capabilities. This is not an excuse for communicating less; rather, it means communicating more genuinely on a deeper level that further builds trust. Those who seek to be the fount of all wisdom and dispenser of all power are not leaders; they are megalomaniacs, limited by the scope of their own ideas and the span of their own control. In contrast, leaders are those who want to share the responsibilities, seek input from all quarters, want contributions from everyone, and actively encourage others to step forward to manage and lead. In other words, they are good motivators.

## Insights into Motivation: David McGregor

David McGregor, a social psychologist, developed motivational theories that have come to be known as Theory X and Theory Y. Theory X holds that people are lazy and must be compelled to work. As a result, people need to be "coerced, directed and threatened." Furthermore, the workers want to be told what to do because they lack "ambition" and "want to avoid responsibility." In short, it's the "carrot and stick" theory of human motivation. Theory Y is the direct opposite. It describes people as willing to work when they are given good reasons to do so. As a result, workers will produce when they can achieve and "seek responsibility."[4] McGregor did not view these theories as "mutually exclusive"; organizations are a blend of the two. In fact, he was working on something he called Theory Z, which was a "synthesis" of his thinking.[5]

## Motivation Planner: Empower

Empowering is the art of handing off responsibility and authority to others so that they can do the work. Use the following questions to see how you can establish a more empowered workplace.

Empowerment is about preparing people both to contribute and to lead. Consider the following.

1. What opportunities exist in your organization for people to demonstrate their leadership skills? What challenges can you provide that will help them grow and develop their talents and skills?

2. How can you give more responsibility to people on your team? Identify candidates and consider their strengths and opportunities for growth. How will this new assignment help them grow?

3. How can you make it known to others that you have granted authority for a specific project to a specific person? Will you do this in a meeting, by e-mail, or in some other way? Be specific.

4. How can you hold people accountable for their actions? How will you point out the consequences of succeeding or not succeeding? How will you make yourself available without undercutting their authority?

5. How will your encourage your direct reports to empower their people?

## SAM WALTON

If you want to motivate an entrepreneur, you tell him no. That's what happened to Sam Walton in 1962 when he opened his first discount store. Men in suits traveled from Chicago to Arkansas and said, "Don't build any more of these Wal-Mart stores." It was not an idle threat. Sam Walton ran a chain of successful Ben Franklin variety stores, and the men at Ben Franklin headquarters did not want one of their franchisees branching out into a competitive business. Within a year, Wal-Mart no. 1, the first store, was doing nearly a million dollars in sales, dwarfing the sales of his Ben Franklins, which were earning $200,000 to $300,000 annually.[6]

## NOT ONE TO BACK DOWN

Adversity did not frighten Sam Walton. Born in Kingfisher, Oklahoma, in 1918, he had seen the hard side of life. He had accompanied his father through Depression-era Oklahoma when his father had to foreclose on farms. He had lived through his parents' unhappy marriage; they separated when he was in college. He had paid his way through college by working at a couple of jobs. And he had been rejected for overseas duty by the army, despite being a top cadet in ROTC at the University of Missouri. He had also suffered as a businessman. He opened his first Ben Franklin in 1945 and turned it into a money-maker. However, much to his chagrin, he had signed only a five-year lease on the building, and the landlord would not renew, so he was forced to give up the business and move. It was a painful move; he and his wife, Helen, were well established in Newport, Arkansas, and uprooting his business and his family was very hard. Not one to look back, however, Walton opened Walton's Five and Dime in Bentonville, a town 175 miles away and half the size. That store proved successful, and he opened a number of other stores before he opened his first Wal-Mart and then many more, eventually building the world's largest retailer.[7]

## COMPETITIVE CURIOSITY

Growing big was not Walton's dream; giving the customer great value, more for less, was his mantra. After all, how high could a man in his position in rural Arkansas in 1962 dream of going in retailing? Sears was the dominant mass merchant, followed by a few national chains, including Kmart, Woolco, and Target—the last three established by rich parent companies (S.S. Kresge, F.W. Woolworth, and Dayton-Hudson, respectively) in 1962, the same year that the first Wal-Mart opened. Walton was not even the only discounter; there were scads of them all over the South. Herb Gibson was a notable discounter. The smaller discounters did not last; as Sam Walton noted, they succumbed to the temptations of wealth—fancy cars, jets, and yachts.[8] As historian Richard Tedlow notes, they lost their "discipline," which he says is the essence of retail success.[9] Kmart and Woolco suffered similar fates, although it was years before their slack operations caught up with them.[10]

As an up-and-comer, however, Walton borrowed merchandising ideas from the best. His relentless curiosity drove him to visit competitive stores, chat up the managers, mix and mingle with corporate retail heads, and write everything down. One manager from Wal-Mart's early days recalls Walton urging his managers to do the same—shop the competition with an open mind. That is, Walton wanted to know what his competitors were doing right as well as what they were doing wrong. And if something was a good idea, he borrowed it. In fact, Walton Five and Dime was only the nation's third self-service variety store; in 1950 he was well ahead of his time. His curiosity was combined with his competitive spirit; he was learning from anyone and everyone so that he could become a better competitor. Certainly he burned to beat the best, but he turned his competition into value for the customer. He sought to buy direct wherever he could and turn it with a slim margin. The old discount mantra of "buy low, stack high, and sell cheap" served him well.[11] Walton was not unique in this; in fact, every discounter was doing it. What differentiated Wal-Mart was Sam Walton as motivator.

"Walton was a born leader…," says historian Richard Tedlow. "Walton led by example." Tedlow notes the now-famous episode of Sam Walton dancing the hula on Wall Street because he had lost a bet to the CEO, David Glass; the bet was over whether Wal-Mart would deliver a "pre-tax profit of greater than

8 percent [which] it did." As Tedlow points out, Walton could have fired Glass, but he chose to honor his commitment and live up to his end of the bargain. Although as a merchandiser, he and his team had done wild stunts before, he had never done them so publicly. Still, when Sam Walton made a bet, he abided by it.[12]

## PARTNERSHIP FOR SUCCESS

In his autobiography, *Made in America*, Walton attributes Wal-Mart's success to his employees. "What has carried this company this far so fast is the unbelievable relationship that we, the managers, have been able to enjoy with our associates," whom he defines as hourly employees. "Our relationship with the associates is a partnership in the truest sense. It's the only reason our company has been able to outperform the competition—and even our own expectations."[13] If this is true, then the partnership did not begin on the best of footings, largely because, as Walton says, "I was so chintzy." His wife, Helen, who was a life partner in the truest sense, recalls advocating better pay for the hourly workers, a view that she says her husband "didn't appreciate."[14] He did, however, change his tune. He was one of the first to make rank-and-file employees eligible for profit sharing, a change in status that made many thousands of employees millionaires.

And along with sharing the wealth, Walton opened the books. He wanted his employees to run the business as if it were their own. While headquarters dictated strict logistical and operational controls, Walton wanted store managers and department managers to think like owners. He opened the books so that people could see how they were doing as well as how the whole company was doing. Walton wanted people to merchandise as he might; their promotions were creative and drew thousands to the stores. Retail is about excitement, and Wal-Mart knew how to create excitement with special promotions on top of everyday low prices. Walton drove decision making to the front lines, and he says that one of his greatest satisfactions was when he heard a manager talking about her performance and saying that she was number five, but she wanted to move up to number one.[15] His competitive fire was contagious.

One reason for the contagion was that Sam Walton spread it. His one luxury in life, if it really was a luxury, was flying; he owned 18 airplanes (all of which he bought used) and flew them himself to scout possible store sites as well as visit his stores. He spoke to the associates as one of them; he dispelled any sense of awe about himself. Said one manager about Walton, "He is a master at erasing that 'larger than life' feeling that people have for him. How many [leaders] always start the conversation by wanting to know what *you* think? What's on *your* mind?" The manager also said, "It's almost like having your oldest friend come just to see if you're okay. He never let us down."[16] No doubt Walton had his detractors, but that assessment lays bare two keys to Walton's ability to motivate: one, he asked people for their opinions first, and two, he connected with them on a personal level. Any leader who can do that will be able to lead his people anywhere. And there is a third element: respect. Sam Walton was in his heart a simple, decent man who respected people and sought to treat them square and let them know it. "[T]here's no better way to keep someone doing things the right way than by letting him or her know how much you appreciate their performance. . . . Human nature will take it from there."[17]

The other thing that made Walton so popular was his accessibility. The man who succeeded Walton as CEO, David Glass, points out that it was "not unusual" for employees to drive to Bentonville unannounced to meet with Walton. Glass rhetorically asks, "How many chairmen of $50 billion companies do you know who are totally, 100 percent accessible to their hourly associates?" Walton also had great faith in people. He tells a story in *Made in America* about an urban store in Dallas that was suffering from "shrinkage," i.e., theft. A new manager was put in, and the shrinkage rate dropped to less than the national average. The new manager had succeeded in making this turnaround because, like Sam, he treated the employees fairly and went out of his way to demonstrate ways of success: recognizing employees who did well, making a hero of a woman who had caught a thief leaving with merchandise, and raising the employees' expectations of what they could do. The story is all the more powerful because the manager did it by following Sam's example. That's when you know your culture is contagious.[18]

As Wal-Mart has emerged as the world's largest retailer, and in fact the world's largest company, its culture has frayed. It has become the target of thousands of employee lawsuits and class action suits over unfair labor practices and sexual discrimination.[19] It would be comforting to think that such things would not occur under Sam's watch, but reality might dictate that when a company becomes too big, it may not be able to maintain its cohesive culture, something that Walton had always tried to foster. Still, Walton's life is worthy of study, and his example is one from which everyone from entrepreneurs to entry-level employees can learn.

## RULES FOR SUCCESS

Sam Walton offered some rules for business success; of the ten he included in his autobiography, six focused on motivation, one using that word and the other five demonstrating how to motivate: spread the wealth, communicate, listen, appreciate, and celebrate.[20] Each of those steps was something that he practiced himself and expected his senior managers and store managers to practice as well. In fact, all of them come together in a Wal-Mart tradition: the Saturday morning get-together. Every Saturday, Wal-Mart managers gather to share information, recognize "heroes" (those employees who merit mention), do goofy things (this is retail, after all), and sing the Wal-Mart cheer. Corny? You betcha, but it works for Wal-Mart. A more extended version of this get-together takes place at the annual shareholders' meeting, now held in the Bud Walton Arena (named for Sam's younger brother and partner). Once a simple meeting, today it's a week-long extravaganza where shareholders meet and mingle with executives and employees. During Sam's lifetime, employees would gather at his home for barbecue, with Sam serving not only as host but as inquisitive merchandiser: "How we doing at Litchfield, Illinois?"[21] Wal-Mart was family to Sam, not simply because his own family was involved (notably his brother and his son, Rob), but because he viewed his managers and associates as family, people with whom he visited and socialized and from whom he learned.

When Sam Walton died of cancer on April 5, 1992, Wal-Mart's annual revenues were around $44 billion. Many predicted that the company was at its high-water mark and would decline. What skeptics did not understand was that Sam Walton had handed off the operations to David Glass and his team. Rob Walton, Sam's eldest son, became chairman, but no one, not even Rob, tried to pretend to be Sam. The Walton family, still the largest shareholder, remains engaged in the company but does not actively run its operation. Lee Scott, Glass's successor as CEO, put it this way: "We're not made up of celebrities. It's the way it all comes together that is our strength."[22] Add in the partnership with associates and you have Sam's formula for a legacy.

---

## Leadership Lessons in Motivation

- *Live for competition*. Sam Walton was a relentless competitor. From his school days to his entrepreneurial years, he loved to compete himself, and he enabled his team to compete along with him.

- *Be curious*. Sam Walton was someone who loved to see what the competition was up to and to question and query his competition. He expected the same of his people.

- *Recognize and promote talent*. Sam Walton had an eye for choosing people who had his capacity for hard work as well as his discipline and competitive

(*Continued on next page.*)

> spirit. While he recruited from outside the organiza-
> tion, he also groomed talent from within.
>
> - *Share the wealth.* Profit sharing enabled Sam Walton
>   to make his employees owners. They, like him, had a
>   stake in the business and would run it accordingly.
> - *Live the values.* Sam Walton was fabulously wealthy,
>   but he lived simply. He exuded the common touch,
>   and people loved him for it.

## EARVIN "MAGIC" JOHNSON

Where to begin? For many people, their earliest recollection of Magic Johnson is as a lanky college sophomore point guard who led Michigan State to victory in the 1979 NCAA basketball finals. The touted duel between Magic and Larry Bird, who was playing in his final game for Indiana State, never materialized; MSU cruised to victory. The next season, in the pros, Magic gained instant stardom as an NBA player. His winning smile and sheer exuberance could not be denied. In fact, during his first game as a pro, he leapt into the arms of a startled Kareem Abdul-Jabbar, who had made the winning shot at the buzzer. That was not "cool" by NBA standards, but Magic's enthusiasm, coupled with his extraordinary play at point guard, helped the Lakers to their first NBA title in years.[23] It was to be the first of five titles with Magic at point, the master choreographer of Laker Show-time, up-tempo buzzer-beating basketball that rocked the league and put fans in the seats.

Then, almost as suddenly as it had begun, it was over. Magic Johnson strode to the podium at the Forum, where the Lakers played, and announced that he was retiring—in the prime of his career. He was only 32 years old. The reason: He had acquired HIV. While he was not ill, he had been advised to take a year off and see if he could strengthen his immunity. It was said then that suddenly everyone in America knew someone who had the AIDS virus. And if people thought Magic was through, that only proved their ignorance of his drive, his commitment, and his sheer enthusiasm. They also were not listening; he said then, "I plan on living for a long time. . . . Life is going to go on for me, and I'm going to be a happy man."[24] His basketball career was largely over (he did return for a brief encore, and he did play on the vaunted 1992 U.S. Olympic Dream Team), but his career as an entrepreneur was only beginning. Magic Johnson was just getting started.

## HUMBLE ROOTS

Born in 1959 in Lansing, Michigan, the fourth of seven children, Earvin Johnson grew up in very modest circumstances. The value of hard work was instilled in him at an early age. His father worked in a GM plant making Buicks and usually worked a second job to help make ends meet. While his father's hobby was fixing up old cars, young Earvin found his own passion—basketball. From a young age he was a good player, but while the fundamentals of the game came easily to him, the fundamentals of education needed to be drilled.[25]

In his autobiography, *My Life*, Johnson recalls a teacher in elementary school, Mrs. Dart, "benching" him from playing in a recreation-league championship game because he had failed to turn in a homework assignment. While Mrs. Dart may have had no legal authority to prevent him from playing, she had influence; she called his parents and his coach. Johnson missed the championship game. While he was infuriated at the time, he learned a valuable life lesson about the importance of education. The incident, says Johnson, drew him closer to Mrs. Dart and later her husband, who was an amateur-league coach.[26]

Johnson learned about racial divisions from his father, who was born in Mississippi and would take the family South on vacations. He recalls his father insisting that his children say "Yes, sir" and "No, sir" when speaking to white people. In fact, Magic recalls being in Mississippi in 1990 when a white man his father's age approached him and said, "Boy, you play basketball, don't you?" Earvin Johnson "held his temper" at the word *boy*, remembering what his father had always said, "that we shouldn't forget these people had come a long, long, way."[27]

Earvin Johnson confronted racism at home in Michigan when he was bused to Everett, a predominantly white school in Lansing. He was an easygoing fellow, and he mixed easily with white and black students; he recalls that he used his persuasive skills with the school principal to have some "black music," along with "white rock music," piped into the school lunchroom. On the basketball court, however, he did not meet with a friendly reception. During practice he was "frozen out" by the white players, who kept the ball from him. He challenged them in an angry confrontation that his coach had to mediate. After the confrontation, the situation mellowed, and Earvin emerged as the team's point guard—in essence, the team quarterback.[28]

It was as a high school freshman that he earned his nickname. After a spectacular game in which he recorded his first "triple-double" (double digits in points, rebounds, and assists), a reporter from the *Lansing State Journal* congratulated him on his outstanding performance. The reporter said that something was missing, however—a nickname. And so it was that Fred Stabley, Jr., gave him the name by which the city of Lansing, the state of Michigan, and the whole world would eventually know him— Magic! It was not a name his mother liked or approved of. As Magic says, when someone uses the name in her presence, she corrects it by saying, "Earvin" or "Junior." Humility was something that he learned from his mother. But there was something else that he got from her: the smile! And it is that radiant smile of his that seems to affirm the rightness of his nickname, Magic, his mother's objections notwithstanding.[29]

## LESSONS FROM THE GAME

Magic was a highly recruited basketball player, but he chose to stay close to home, enrolling in Michigan State, in neighboring East Lansing. As a player he was an immediate sensation, helping Michigan State capture a Big Ten title. Expectations for his sophomore season were no less high. The team, under the direction of coach Jud Heathcote, did not disappoint.

Magic was the undisputed team leader, but it was a position that he earned. His father had taught him how to play tough and not be distracted by calls that went against him or by the physical play of others. A high-energy player, Magic played with gamelike intensity in practice as well as in games. As a point guard, Magic ran the floor; he told his players where to be, and he got them the ball. He played selflessly, preferring to dish the ball to a teammate, letting the player score while taking the assist for himself. He also pounded the boards hard, capturing a high percentage of rebounds. He was a point guard, but his rebound average was that of a power forward. His 6'9" height helped him establish position, but his keen sense of where the ball would go served him even better. And when it came to crunch time, Magic could score; he could light up the court as well as anyone. Magic Johnson redefined the position of point guard as a genuine triple threat—assisting, rebounding, and scoring. He was the consummate team leader, the "go-to guy" who could make things happen.

When Michigan State rolled into the finals against the number-one-ranked team, Indiana State, with the number-one collegiate player, Larry Bird, it was a showdown that people had waited for. To this day, more than 25 years after the game was played in March 1979, it remains the highest-rated NCAA basketball final game. It was the game that brought the NCAA Final Four to prominence. Heathcote devised a scheme to slow Larry Bird and had a player shadow him at all times. Michigan State, playing as a team under Magic's guidance, cruised to victory. While Bird scored a respectable 19 points, a broken thumb and a stingy defense hindered him.[30]

While the game was the last collegiate game for both Bird and Magic, who decided to enter the NBA draft early, it marked the beginning of a relationship between the two that took the NBA by storm and ushered in a new era. Just as the two had electrified the NCAA finals, they soon electrified the NBA. With

Bird playing for the Boston Celtics and Magic playing for the Los Angeles Lakers, a bicoastal rivalry was established. Every time the two met, it was a battle, reminiscent of the Wilt Chamberlain versus Bill Russell duels. Three times in the eighties the two teams met in the finals, with Boston winning once and the Lakers twice. Bird, like Magic, was a team player who could take over a game all by himself. Not surprisingly, the two did not start out as friends, but during the shooting of a television commercial, they spent time together and discovered that they had much in common. Chick Hearn, the late long-time announcer for the Los Angeles Lakers, used to say that when Magic and Bird were on their games, they would not let their teams lose. Such ability is rare, but it breeds a confidence within a team that makes it better as a team, and so the team does become unbeatable.[31]

Bird and Magic also did something else: They brought out the best in each other. As rivals, they spurred each other to greater heights. Bird won three MVP trophies before Magic won his first. Magic's teams won five NBA titles; Larry Bird's teams won three. In short, they motivated each other to play hard, play to win, and play for keeps. Both players put everything into the game on the court. And so it is no wonder that they remain friends. Magic muses in *My Life* that he sees a time when he and Bird will be old men playing checkers. And he adds, "I'd whip his ass."[32]

## AIDS ACTIVISM

But would Magic ever become old? That was the question that haunted everyone when he announced to the world that he was HIV-positive. Immediately rumors that Magic might be homosexual arose. Magic did not run from the spotlight. The same intensity that he displayed on the court, he displayed in fighting back against disease. It was a double-pronged crusade. On one level, Magic undertook a regimen of drug therapies that enabled him to become nearly virus-free. On another level, he championed AIDS-related causes, even serving on a presidential commission established by George H. W. Bush. Magic's focus was on education.

In denying homosexual liaisons, he made it crystal clear that he had gotten the virus through promiscuous sex.

Magic brought AIDS out of the closet. Speaking on the tenth anniversary of Magic's public announcement, Hattie Battie, executive director of AIDS Action, said, "Ten years ago, it was seen as particularly a gay disease. Magic having been so forthcoming . . . helped the rest of society come to grips with it as a disease that affects every community."[33] Dr. Alexandra Levine, a veteran AIDS researcher at the University of Southern California, agrees. "[Magic] brought me the ability to speak to much wider audiences than before, and especially with young people. It was always a concern to me that without education, [HIV/AIDS] would take control. The announcement from Magic Johnson allowed us greater credibility. . . . Educators were more accepting of discussion of sexual things and so forth."[34] While Dr. Levine was speaking of education specific to Los Angeles, her testament to Magic's impact on AIDS awareness applied nationwide, if not worldwide. Magic himself takes the education process to heart. "When I first came back to the league [for a comeback], players were running scared. It took the first five years to really educate people." Today Magic is focusing on the black community. "Black women are the fastest-rising group getting the disease. So, I'm speaking out to black women as well as black males." Johnson understands that while the rates of contraction for gays have declined, numbers have risen in the "minority heterosexual community." He knows he can play an active role in stemming that tide. There is much more to do, he acknowledges.[35]

The other thing that Johnson demonstrates is optimism. "I don't feel ill," he said in September 2002 when he was about to be inducted into the NBA Basketball Hall of Fame. "I never have. I still work out every day like I normally do. . . . Maybe God just had a plan for me and wanted me to be around for a little while longer. I am a person that meets challenges head on, and I've done everything I'm supposed to do. I didn't stop living because I was diagnosed with HIV. My attitude has been super."[36] His incandescent smile attests to his relentless positivism.

One way in which Earvin Johnson is educating is by giving back to his community through the Magic Johnson Foundation. Established in 1991, the foundation started as a "single-disease organization . . . to raise funds . . . for HIV/AIDS education and prevention programs." Today the purpose of the organization has expanded, as needs in the urban community have increased, to "address all aspects of our youth's lives." The foundation serves as a source of funding for nonprofit organizations that are working to improve the lives of disadvantaged children in urban areas.[37]

## BUSINESS ACUMEN

*Super* is a word that you can apply to Earvin Johnson's career in business. It was not a career that began when his basketball career ended. In fact, he had been preparing for it for quite some time. "Power comes from ownership, and until blacks start owning more businesses and supporting those businesses, thing aren't going to change," he wrote in *My Life*. "But the road to that goal runs through college."[38] Although he left college early, he returned in the summer to finish his degree, as he had promised his mother he would. He also sought the mentorship of some powerful business figures in Los Angeles. And he listened to what they advised him. One was Michael Ovitz, the founder of Creative Artists Agency and a one-time Disney executive. He urged Magic to get educated in business, suggesting that he read the *Wall Street Journal* daily along with other trade publications. One reason Magic respected Ovitz was that Ovitz did not defer to his stardom; as a Hollywood power broker, Ovitz was in fact a star himself and so didn't need Magic's aura in order to shine. Ovitz negotiated an endorsement contract with Pepsi under which Magic would also get a stake in a Pepsi distributorship.[39]

That was only the beginning. Johnson soon emerged as an entrepreneur. His first major venture was to establish Magic Theater, a nationwide chain of movie theaters located in inner-city neighborhoods. Together with Janet Jackson and a record executive, he purchased a bank and made it the first black-owned national bank. He also owns TGI Fridays and Starbucks franchises, all of which he locates in urban neighborhoods. In addition, he has a business relationship with Lincoln Mercury to help market its product line to urban consumers. By bringing national chains and national brands to urban neighborhoods, his company, Johnson Development, is accomplishing multiple missions. One, it is providing good products to paying customers who have not had these choices in their neighborhoods. Two, he is providing jobs and career paths to local men and women who have been shut out of mainstream jobs. And three, he is giving something that all good motivators give: hope. Earvin Johnson is a celebrity black man who transcended the color line not simply as an athlete (many have done that), but as an entrepreneur. Johnson is winning in a world from which people of color have been excluded, and he is winning big.[40]

## THE LEGACY

"What I just tried to do was be the best player that I could, but also the best winner that I could," said Johnson said on the eve of being inducted into the Hall of Fame. "The only thing that I wanted to do in basketball was win. I wasn't faster than a lot of guys. I couldn't jump as high. What I was, I was very intelligent, very smart player. And I loved to play. I not only played for my teammates and for Los Angeles, but for the fans. I loved to get them going."[41]

The legacy of Magic Johnson the player exists in the videotape archives of ESPN and the NBA Hall of Fame in Springfield, Massachusetts, as well as in the memories of his many fans at Michigan State and in Los Angeles. The legacy of Earvin "Magic" Johnson, the founder of Johnson Development Company and the Magic Johnson Foundation, is being written across the urban landscape of America as he seeks to make the world safer as well as more hospitable for young men and women with dreams such as his. Hang on; it just might be another "Showtime"!

## Lessons in Leadership Motivation

- *Demonstrate enthusiasm*. Earvin "Magic" Johnson invites people to share his joy in what he does. His radiant smile is a mirror of his sharing soul.

- *Work hard at your craft.* Magic Johnson practiced hard on the court. Earvin Johnson schooled himself in the ways of business so that he could one day build his own business.

- *Share the load*. Magic Johnson was the consummate team player. He enabled others on the team to score and share in the limelight.

- *Lead the team.* Magic Johnson stepped forward in crucial situations to lead his team to victory. He enabled players to play above themselves in order to win as a team.

- *Leverage your strengths to help others*. Earvin Johnson uses his celebrity status to raise awareness of the problems of urban youth. He uses his entrepreneurial skills to create opportunities for people in the inner city to join the mainstream as wage earners and contributors to society.

"I'd much prefer that the team be accountable to each other than to me. It's a far more powerful method of team-building."

*Pat Summitt*
*Head coach, Tennessee Lady Volunteers*

# COACH

## AN UNCONVENTIONAL COACH

*H*E IS THE CHIEF STOCKHOLDER *in an imvestment company with huge ownership stakes in many of this country's biggest companies. His advice is sought by politicians, potentates, and CEOs the world over. They come to his hometown for a little one-on-one time with the shrewdest investor in Omaha, if not the universe. There is little pretension about the second-richest man in America. When VIP guests come to visit, he picks them up at the airport in his own car, a late-model Lincoln Town Car that anyone on a modest* *salary could easily afford. He is Warren Buffett, whose wealth is measured in tens of billions and whose advice is worth even more.*[1]

*In the latter years of his career, Buffett has emerged as something of a coach. While he is close-mouthed about his sessions, we do know something about the advice he gave to one of his most famous friends, Katharine Graham. When she decided to take the Washington Post Company public, Berkshire Hathaway took a stake in the new company, and in the process Buffett emerged as her trusted adviser. His financial advice was no doubt of keen value; the newly public company prospered. But his personal advice was of more value to Graham; he believed in her leadership, and that faith was precious to her.*[2]

*The faith that Buffett exhibited toward Graham is the faith that he demonstrates to all CEOs he believes in. What he gives CEOs, who include the heads of General Electric, Disney, Bank One, and Xerox, is straight talk over steaks at his favorite restaurant. In an era when all too many people are afraid to tell it like it is to their boss, Buffett can shoot straight from the hip. He understands both the management and the investor side of issues; he typically sides with investors, whose point of view is something that CEOs need to hear.*

*Perhaps the friendship that has sparked the most interest (as well as intrigue among business journalists) is the one he enjoys with Bill Gates, the founder of Microsoft and the world's richest man. Something of a mentor to Gates, Buffett has helped Gates evolve beyond geekdom into a respected business leader in his own right. There is a funny story told about the two in Omaha; they had stopped for ice cream somewhere when Buffett's car suffered engine trouble. Here they were, the two richest businessmen in the world, stranded in the middle of nowhere eating ice cream. Humbling? Certainly not for Buffett. One gets the sense that he does not take his wealth and power too seriously.*

*While Buffett will not travel for bigwigs, he will make a trek for students. According to the* Wall Street Journal, *he awarded each member of a class he guest lectured to at the University of*

*Tennessee a share of stock in Berkshire Hathaway, worth $2,700.
And like the true coach that he is, he remains a teacher. "Students
aren't fully formed and are often more willing to listen and
learn."[3] The counsel and advice that Buffett shares with students
and CEOs alike is akin to the example of his own mentor, Ben-
jamin Graham, who taught young Warren at Columbia.*

✍ ✍

There is a story told by a pair of Harvard psychologists and professors, James Waldroop and Timothy Butler, who work in the
placement office of the Harvard Business School. Year after
year, students returning to Harvard tell their professors that
when they were in school, they loved doing the quantitative
work that required empirical thinking based upon facts. As students, they paid little attention to the human dynamics that were
taught to them. As Waldroop and Butler say in their book, *The
12 Bad Habits That Hold Good People Back*, these former students, now well entrenched in the workforce and having risen to
leadership positions, say that they wish they had spent more
time on the "soft stuff" because that's what's important for
achieving the intended results.[4] The cliché, "The soft stuff is the
hard stuff," referring to managing people, is more true than
ever. As more and more companies outsource everything but
their core competencies, what matters most is what organizations do well. And to do anything well, whether it be construc-
tion, design, manufacturing, science, or social service, you
need to have good people. And you had better treat those people well because they can walk out the door, leaving your enterprise high and dry.

Those organizations that succeed in managing their people
well do so by positioning their managers as coaches. As Marcus
Buckingham and Curt Coffman emphasize in their seminal book
on management best practices, *First, Break All the Rules*, people
join companies but leave bosses. Successful managers are those
who create an environment in which people can contribute and

achieve and in which they are supported in their efforts. As a result, they are well motivated and wish to remain in their organization.[5] Jim Plunkett succeeded because of his skill on the field, but also because of his ability to lead his team; other players trusted him because he connected to them on a personal level. Likewise Warren Buffett may be a financial genius, but it is his ability to relate to his managers and the managers of the companies he owns that brings people to him. Each in his own way, Plunkett on the field and Buffett in the boardroom, coaches his people to succeed.

## CULTURE OF COACHING

There is another salient feature of high-performing organizations: They have all developed a culture of coaching. Such a culture places a premium on developing people in the workplace so that they can utilize their talents and skills to achieve short- and long-term goals for themselves, their teams, and their organizations. These cultures are people-centric; they know that their success is based upon the people they have, and they treat those people right. Think of a professional football team. Every man on the roster has a significant role to play; there are only 53 to suit up for a given game, which may seem like a lot given that only 11 play at a time, but because of the ferocity of the game, injuries are a common occurrence. It is becoming less common for a team to have a single quarterback for the entire season. These players are trained well, conditioned well, fed well, and travel first class, and as a result, they are expected to play hard and play to win. If they do not play up to expectations, either because they do not execute the plays or because they get out of condition, they are released. With one hand, they are coddled; with the other hand (or, better yet, foot), they are booted.

Few workplaces are as rigorous or as hard-edged, but by examining a competitive professional football team, you can see both sides of the management culture in microcosm: soft versus hard. A coaching culture puts a premium on people. In football, you cannot play without players; in management, you cannot do the work without employees. Coaches do not play; managers do not perform the skilled labor—that is, the engineering, the design, the assembly, the nursing, the doctoring, the physical laboring. What coaches and managers do is get other people to do the work and help them do it. Pat Summitt's approach to coaching is intense; her intensity, coupled with her conviction and her belief in her players, enables her team to succeed year after year, contending for national championships. Summitt unlocks the competitive spirit in her players and leverages that inner spark to challenge her players to succeed. In other words, she is raising their expectations of themselves.

In high-performing organizations, managers are like servants to the workers; they provide them with the training, the tools, the development, and, yes, the opportunity to do the work and do it well. The work of a manager, like that of a coach, is to encourage production so that everyone in the organization benefits. Therefore, managers who take on the role of coach are managers who achieve some of the greatest rewards. Their teams produce, and their psyches are soothed because they have done something good and noble: They have helped others to achieve. Creating a culture of coaching is really creating a culture in which people are motivated. Here are some things to do to develop such a culture.

- *Make expectations clear.* The era of performance appraisal in which we now live has compelled managers to set performance objectives. This is a good thing. Unfortunately, many performance objectives are written cryptically or the situations have changed, making the objectives moot, with the result that employees are still in the dark about what they are supposed to do. Managers need to be explicit about what they expect in terms of output, but they also need to be clear about what they expect in terms of the human side. Managers have a right and a duty to expect employees to be timely, to dress appropriately, and to collaborate with coworkers. Likewise, employees have a right to expect managers to supply them with the time and resources they need to do the job and to inform them how to do the job well. When Magic Johnson was playing basketball, he had high expectations for himself, but also for his teammates. His hard work, especially in practice, challenged the other players to follow his example. And during the games, he expected them to follow his instructions; as the point guard, he was the on-court coach.

- *Provide feedback.* One reason why employees feel that they are in the dark is that their managers are uncommunicative. If an employee does not hear something negative, she assumes that all is well. Managers need to let people know how they are doing. One manager with whom I worked used reports submitted to him as occasions for giving feedback; he would write observations in the margins that were specific to the report as well as specific to the individual. It takes time to give feedback, but it is a terrific way to help people develop their talents. Colleen Barrett and her team at Southwest Airlines believe in feedback as a learning tool; people need it if they are to grow and develop their talents.

- *Create a work development plan.* The world in which we work is changing more rapidly than we would like, so it is a truism that in order to keep on doing what you are doing, you need to upgrade your skills. Managers can work with employees to develop work plans designed to keep the employees up to date with technical information and provide opportunities for growth within the job. Pfizer, the pharmaceutical giant, uses work plans to provide its people with a combination of technical training and skills development. Managers can also create job rotations and project leadership assignments as growth opportunities.

- *Consider a career plan.* Every employee should be thinking about where she will go next in the organization. Once upon a time, companies did all the career thinking for their employees. Today employees need to take ownership of the process, but managers must take an active role. Incorporate career planning into performance reviews. By doing this, the manager is nudging the employee to take the initiative. Wal-Mart executives have only to look around to see their careers; most senior leaders on the operations side have come up through the ranks, something that Sam Walton encouraged.

- *Teach coaching behavior.* Coaching is integral to management. Managers who coach are modeling the correct behaviors, and many organizations now include coaching in the executive development process. It works well not only for employees who are assuming first-line managerial slots, but also for more senior managers, who may not have benefited from coaching during their career. Some of the best teachers of coaches are managers. Why? Because they know the culture and the challenges that emerging leaders face. Recruit managers for the development programs. Thich Nhat Hanh is a born teacher. In his talks and his writings, he shares his insights into how to become better parents, friends, colleagues, and even leaders.

- *Mentor.* Mentoring is a form of coaching in that it works to develop talents and skills, but it really is different. The purpose of mentoring is to provide guidance over the long term in order to help the mentee acquire knowledge and skills and network throughout the organization. Think of mentors as great-uncles; they know you, but not as intimately as a parent or grandparent does. An ideal mentor is disinterested; that is, the performance of the mentee does not reflect on the mentor's performance. The concept of mentoring comes from the academic community, where seasoned professors take Ph.D. candidates under their wing and advise them through the rigors of the thesis and qualifying for professorships. In the corporate arena, it may include senior leaders adopting high-potential managers as assistants or meeting with them regularly to help nurture their careers. Trade associations also offer mentoring, pairing senior and junior people; often these individuals work for different organizations, so there is total disinterest at the outset.

All of these steps individually and collectively improve the work environment. As a result, they lay the foundation for motivation at all levels of the organization.

## WANTING TO DO THE WORK

Coaching is a key leadership behavior. It also is a key, or maybe even *the* key, to creating a workplace where people want to come to work, want to do their work, and want to be recognized for their contributions—in other words, a workplace where people are motivated. Part of the reason for their motivation is the fact that their manager makes it known that he values them as people and as contributors. He knows them personally; he knows whom to ask about family matters and whom not to. He knows their hobbies, and he knows those whose hobby is work. He knows their expectations and their aspirations. In other words, he knows them as fully dimensional human beings, not automatons who come to work and while away the hours like drones. And, in return, they know him and, even better, respect him. Why? Because he has taken the time to invest a part of himself in each of them. That is not something you do overnight; you do it over time—weeks, months, and years.

Often those people who shy away from coaching are those who have never been coached themselves. Men especially feel awkward in dealing with the human dimension. As a result, they put up walls between themselves and their workers that prevent genuine communication. The workplace is not a group therapy session, and it is not a family, no matter how much people proclaim that it is. It is a place that is ideally designed for the production of something, be it ideas, services, products, or processes. Such a workplace is measured by output, and if the output is not sufficient given the time and resources, tough decisions must be made. People may be let go and replaced with new people. Good coaches do not shy away from such responsibility; they handle these decisions with dignity and honor. They explain what went right and what went wrong, and they often try to help the individuals move on to the next step. Dealing with the soft stuff can be hard, really gut-wrenchingly hard, but someone has to make the decisions. Managers as coaches can do it and will do it.

## COACHING MATTERS

Coaching, be it in sports or management, is a hard job. It is those who really care about people and results who make the best coaches—not the softies. It is the tough guys and gals who face the facts, work with their people, promote them, and sometimes release them, but overall understand one prime lesson in management: Their success depends upon the success of others. Their job is to nurture, support, grow, and develop those people so that everyone wins, as people and as an organization. That's coaching.

It is the leader's responsibility to coach others so that they can contribute to the team and the organization and better themselves. Coaching requires commitment to the improvement of others. Successful organizations are organizations that make coaching a priority. Motivation emerges from the interest that leaders invest in their people.

### Insights into Motivation: Daniel Goleman

Daniel Goleman, a theorist specializing in organizational behavior, developed the concept of emotional intelligence, or EQ, the ability to relate to and interact with others. Goleman adapted the concept to leadership and developed five attributes: self-awareness (knowing yourself), self-regulation (ability to control your emotions and "think first"), motivation ("passion for work that goes beyond money and status"), empathy (an understanding of others), and social skill (the ability to build relationships with others). Of motivation, Goleman writes that "effective leaders . . . are driven to achieve beyond expectations—their own and everyone else's." A leader with a high degree of emotional intelligence wants to get things done, but done the right way, that is, by bringing people along with her. Such leaders are able to engage the interest and motives of their people as well as create conditions that enable them to succeed.[6]

## Motivation Planner: Coach

Coaching is about bringing out the best in others. Use the following questions to see how you can begin to develop coaching behaviors that will enable people to do their best because they want to excel.

1. How will you make your expectations clear to the employee you are coaching? How will you make your expectations clear to your entire organization (or department)?

2. How often will you provide feedback? How will you give feedback?

3. What steps can you take to create a work development plan for everyone in your organization? Be certain to ask individuals to develop their own plans as a starting point for discussion.

4. When can you discuss career plans with your people? What will you discuss? How will you demonstrate that you want to help them? How will you ensure that they take the initiative in their own career development?

5. Consider opportunities to mentor people outside your department. Invite your employees to mentor new hires.

## PAT SUMMITT

John Maxwell, the noted leadership speaker and author, tells a story about witnessing the University of Tennessee Lady Vols basketball team at halftime. The players filed into the locker room, and the team captains began a discussion at the whiteboard. Someone drew a line down the middle and wrote "1st Half" on one side and "2nd Half" on the other. Then the captains solicited from their team what it had done right during the first half and then what it needed to improve during the second half. After a while the coaches came in, looked at the board, made some remarks and notations on the board, then ushered the team out to the court to play the second half. Dr. Maxwell does not mention whether the Lady Vols won this game, but if they played true to form, they probably did. Under head coach Pat Summitt, the Lady Vols have the highest winning percentage of any women's collegiate basketball team.

Maxwell's story provides a glimpse into how Pat Summitt, year after year, decade after decade, puts her teams into position to win games and championships. By her own admission, Summitt is a taskmaster, a disciplinarian, and a stickler for rules. What she also is, as illustrated by her enabling her team to essentially coach itself at halftime, is supremely confident in her players' abilities and her own coaching style.

## TOUGH LOVE

The Pat Summitt that emerges in her inspirational book, *Reach for the Summit*, is a woman who loves her players as family and who genuinely cares enough about them to push them to their limits with a combination of respect, discipline, challenge, and, most of all, love. Sometimes tough love, but always love. Her example as motivator is masterful because, like all good coaches, she creates the conditions for her players to excel if they want to. And when you play for Summitt, you'd *better* want to. As Abby Conklin, a star player on the 1997 team, put it, "As hard as she is on you when you're on the court, she cares. She teaches more than basketball. She teaches you things that are going to get you through the rest of your life."[7]

Born and raised in rural Henrietta, Tennessee, one of five children with three older brothers, she was a tall, skinny kid, nicknamed "Bones," which she said complemented her sur- name, Head. Her father was a self-made tobacco farmer and dairyman and a stern taskmaster; while she did not get much affection from her father, she did get what she calls "equal opportunity."[8] He demanded that she work just as hard as her brothers, and he expected her to do just as well. Her brothers seemed to fall in with that line, with the result that young "Trish" grew up with great strength as well a strong sense of self.

As a coach, she says she does not ask her players to do any- thing she would not do. That philosophy took root in her days as a player. She played basketball for University of Ten- nessee–Martin as a nonscholarship athlete. (There were no scholarships for women in the pre–Title IX days.) She quali- fied for the U.S. National Team. She later sustained a knee injury, and her rehabilitation took a physical toll (she lost 27 pounds), but her perseverance paid off. She made the first U.S. Olympic women's team and was elected a co-captain. As a starter, she helped her team capture a silver medal in the 1976 Olympic Games.[9]

## BE THE ONE

As coach, you have to want to be in charge. Being a collegiate coach is a huge responsibility. "Oftentimes," Summitt says, "I feel like my heart is on an elevator; it's either lodged in my throat or dropping into my shoes, on their account."[10] She regards her players as "daughters" and has developed close relationships with them over the years, something she treasures. What Summitt expects from her players is respect. In fact, "respect yourself and others" is the first of what she calls her "Definite Dozen," which are her guidelines for playing, coaching, and living. Respect is not imposed. It is earned by leading by example. But you cannot expect it if you do not respect yourself first. That can be "an ongoing process," but it is one that is essential for leading others.[11]

All good coaches are effective communicators, but few are as explicit in their communication as Summitt. She practices three styles of communication. One style is as "confidante and substitute mother." She wants to know her players. In fact, she meets with them one-on-one four times a year to find out how they are doing as athletes, students, and young women. The second style is as a "teacher," who must be firm and stern in her lessons. And the third style is as a game coach, where she "issue[s] blunt commands" and gets her players to "endure adverse situations."[12] This third style is how the world sees her—brash, loud, and sometimes abrasive. She does not make apologies for this; her players know her communication styles. She has learned to control her temper as well as her voice. She does not "condone . . . berating players." If you use "harsh words," you should soften them with appropriate praise. Too much of either is not good for the player or the coach.[13]

Summitt leverages her communication to connect one-to-one with her players. She asks each of her players to take a personality assessment, which she then studies to find out what makes each player tick. As an experienced coach, Summitt can typically predict the personality traits of a young player, but the profile gives her a more accurate insight into the player's psyche. To Summitt, one size does not fit all; all players are different, and she communicates with and challenges each one differently. In other words, she knows which buttons to push. This, of course, drives her players crazy, but at the same time it ideally enables each player to become better at what she does.[14]

Pat Summitt is not about all work and no play. She likes to tell the story of one of her freshman players from Florida, who had never seen snow. The snow began to fall when the Lady Vols were in South Bend for a game, so Summitt drove the young player and a couple of her teammates to an empty parking lot, where she proceeded to throw the car into 360-degree loops, laughing and giggling along the way. As stern as her countenance appears during games, Summitt knows how to keep things loose. One way she does so is by having her son, Tyler, accompany the team. He has formed deep attachments to the players and coaches, but he also keeps things light by acting, well, like a kid. She credits Tyler with loosening her up as a woman and a mother and, in the long run, enabling her to connect better with her players.[15]

## THE FUNDAMENTALS

Summitt has learned to motivate her players by challenging them to achieve what she believes they can achieve for themselves and for the team. She fully realizes that a "love-hate relationship" may evolve and that some players will be at their wit's end trying to figure out how to please her. If things go well, she stays the course; if things deteriorate, she switches her methods.[16] For example, she tells the story of a star player whom she rode hard to get her to produce. Then the young woman went into a shooting slump. Rather than coming down on her, Summitt did the reverse: She comforted her and in the process restored her confidence. Long-time assistant coach Mickie DeMoss says that Summitt is "strategic" in her motivational techniques. Sometimes she gets in a player's face; other times she ignores a player if she "wants kids to think on something." Moss says that Summitt "wants" her players to come back and show her up by proving that she was wrong and that the player can do it.[17]

Teamwork is the essence of championship teams. But teamwork does not just occur; it can be taught. It comes from delegating responsibility to players and incrementally increasing that responsibility over time. It comes from learning to share responsibilities, both offense and defense, on the court as well as off the court. She tells the story of four freshmen and one sophomore who cut classes. Summitt, who has rules about attending class, imposed a penalty on the whole team. Why? It was the upperclassmen's responsibility to ensure that the younger players obeyed the rules.[18]

Rules for Lady Vol players are pretty simple and straightforward: Attend class, sit near the front, and be "vocal" on the court, and "no tattoos may show in public." She admits that the last one is "personal"; tattoos are symbols of "conformity." She wants players who can think and do for themselves—as "leaders."[19] For Summitt, rules are not "arbitrary"; they are designed to enforce expectations and behavior. They also do something else: They create a sense of accountability. As a coach of young women, she knows that rules will be broken, and she enforces them. It is all part of her commitment to discipline. But Summitt is not a martinet; she wants her teams to discipline themselves. That creates an even greater sense of accountability, especially in young adults.[20]

Competition fuels the Lady Vols; it accounts in part for their having won seven NCAA titles. Summitt believes that "competitiveness allows you to influence your opponent."[21] In other words, as General Dwight D. Eisenhower used to say, "What counts is not necessarily the size of the dog in the fight—it's the size of the fight in the dog." And the Lady Vols have plenty of fight. And sometimes it can be personal. Their archrival is the University of Connecticut, which has won five NCAA titles. It is no secret that Summitt and Gino Auriemo, U-Conn's coach, are not the best of friends, or even friendly rivals. But deep down, having a rival like U-Conn only feeds the flames of the Lady Vols' competitive drive. In fact, losing can be therapeutic; after winning three consecutive NCAA titles in the late 1990s, not winning a fourth enabled them to take stock of that "three-peat" and glory in its accomplishment. As a coach, Summitt believes that she must teach a team "how to lose." While losing is very painful, it is instructive, too. "Nothing improves a team, or a person," says Summitt, "more than losing. It forces self-examination; it reveals flaws, and, if you choose to learn from it, it inspires something better."[22]

## STRAIGHT TALKING

What is refreshing about Summitt is her honesty. She refers to herself as a "yeller," one who raises her voice constantly to make certain that she is getting through. She writes that "the greatest strength any human being can have is to recognize her own weaknesses." In this Summitt is truthful to the point of pain. When she became head coach, by default because the head coach quit prior to Summitt's arrival in 1974 at age 22, she says that she was a martinet who barked orders but really did not know how to coach. Later she acknowledges that she has lost players by being too overbearing, or even too hard on herself for not letting up.[23]

Belief plays a significant role in her life. She is a lifelong churchgoer, but she also defines belief as a "practical matter." As a coach, she states, "with a combination of practice and belief, the most ordinary team is capable of extraordinary things." From belief emerges attitude, which is part "emotion and logic." For Summitt, "attitude is a choice. What you *think* you can do."[24] Leaders must believe, and they must project an attitude that balances emotion and logic. She wants her players to adopt the same attitude, and she conveys this through her coaching.[25] As Carla McGhee, who played on two championship teams, puts it, "She's very honest. . . . You have to be that way to stay with her. Once you learn to be honest with her, you have a friend and ally for life."[26]

For more than thirty years, Pat Summitt has been coaching young women basketball players. In *Reach for the Summit*, unlike other books by coaches, you won't find a lot of won-lost statistics. But there is one statistic that stands out among all the others: Every player who has remained at Tennessee has graduated. Many of her players have gone to the professional ranks, but many others have become coaches. Twelve are head coaches in the collegiate ranks. This statistic is something that Summitt openly boasts of because, as she states, she is preparing these young women not only to play, but also to teach and coach. These young women will have the opportunity to do what she has done: have a positive impact on the lives of their players, as students, as young women, and as working professionals.[27] That is influence of the motivating kind.

---

### Lessons in Leadership Motivation

- *Make competition personal.* Pat Summitt stokes the competitive spirit of her players in order to challenge them to take on greater responsibilities.

- *Tailor your communications to the situation.* Pat Summitt communicates to her players as a coach, a teacher, or a confidante, depending on the situation.

- *Connect to each individual as a person.* Pat Summitt discovers what motivates each of her players and connects on that level in order to communicate and coach effectively.

- *Let the team drive the bus.* As a coach, Pat Summitt expects her team to live up to the Lady Vols value system. The team must respect and discipline itself and its members so that they are accountable to each other and the team.

(*Continued on next page.*)

- *Use your beliefs to leverage your strengths*. For Pat Summitt, belief in oneself is essential to success, in competition and in life.
- *Mother your people*. Pat Summitt loves her players as "daughters" and sees it as her responsibility to care and provide for them.

C H A P T E R

"Watching women achieve their dreams is the thing that keeps me inspired."

*Mary Kay Ash*
*Founder, Mary Kay, Inc.*

# RECOGNIZE

## TWO PEOPLE WHO MATTER

*R*ECOGNITION OF US AS HUMAN BEINGS *begins at an early age; we get it first from our parents, siblings, grandparents, and extended family. This is as it should be. But for two generations of Americans, recognition of selfhood began with a man they called Mister Rogers. With a voice as reassuring as a mother's soft hand on a child's cheek and a smile as reassuring as a favorite stuffed toy, Fred Rogers affirmed the dignity of children as people. He entertained them with his songs and skits and his puppet shows; he provided guidance for them on tough subjects like going to school or parental divorce. He was the proverbial* *trusting adult, the one who welcomed us into every show with the cheery, "Hello, neighbor."*

*When he was in a senior in college, Fred Rogers saw something that would change his life forever: television. It was not what he saw on the screen that intrigued him, it was its potential. Upon graduating from Rollins College in 1951 with a degree in musical composition, he made for New York City, where he ended up working at NBC. He then returned home to Pennsylvania and began working for WQED in Pittsburgh, the nation's first public television station, where he created some children's television programming. After a stint working in Canada, he returned to his flagship station with the program that would change the face of the medium,* Mister Rogers' Neighborhood. *He was by then an ordained Presbyterian minister with a mission to work in television. According to his* New York Times *obituary, he articulated his mission as creating a place where children could discover "self-esteem, self-control, imagination, creativity, curiosity . . . tolerance . . . and persistence." For adults, those might be buzzwords; for children, they were a window into growing up.*

*Family and friends said that he was the same person on and off camera, although perhaps more introspective away from the show. He was open and friendly and had a good sense of humor. Eddie Murphy did a recurring send-up of Mister Rogers on* Saturday Night Live. *The first time Fred Rogers met Murphy, he gave him what he gave all the people he liked: a hug.*

*Fred Rogers never preached; he acted. He was an adept puppeteer who created a myriad of recurring characters, all of whom were part of an imaginary world that educated and enchanted children. Few people, men especially, can be said to be nurturers of others outside the home. But* nurturing *is the word that seems to sum up Fred Rogers best. The secret to his technique was a voice that was never raised except in song, a cheering smile, a gift for conversation, and, most of all, an abiding faith in others. Fred Rogers believed in the dignity of our humanity, no matter what our age. While his chief audience was children between the ages of two and six, he was also a favorite of those confined to nursing homes. And it is no wonder that his demeanor awakened in our elders what it did in our children, because, after all, as he said over and over again, "You're special." Is there anything more affirming?*

*His acceptance speech to the Television Hall of Fame in 1999 summed up Fred Rogers's view of his role. "I feel that those of us in television are chosen to be servants. It doesn't matter what our particular job is, we are chosen to help meet the deeper needs of those who watch and listen."*[1]

✍

*For much of her adult life, she was a mother and an active supporter of her husband's career. When he became president, she became something more: a beacon of hope for millions of Americans. She is Betty Ford. For many Americans, "Betty Ford" refers to the clinic that she founded in Palm Springs to treat those with addiction problems. For many other Americans, chiefly women, "Betty Ford" means survivor; during her husband's term in office, she underwent a mastectomy for breast cancer. Both of these events happened in the middle 1970s, when addiction problems and cancer were kept private. That was not Betty Ford's way. She went public as a means of helping others.*

*It was not easy. Making her cancer public was a very personal issue. She recalls coming down the stairs at her first White House reception with her husband, Gerald Ford, after her surgery. "I was very self-conscious . . . and everyone was waiting for us to arrive, I know they were saying, 'Which breast did she say it was?'"*[2] *Mrs. Ford persevered and used the publicity to urge women to be screened for breast cancer. "Without Betty Ford, women would be dying in far greater numbers than they are now," says Zora Brown, founder and president of a breast cancer group.*[3]

*Cancer was one thing; addiction was another. When Betty Ford underwent treatment for abusing painkillers, she characteristically did not shield herself from scrutiny. In fact, she made her story well known in order to raise awareness and to urge others to seek treatment, too. As Mrs. Ford said in a radio interview, "When I got through treatment, I think I thought, 'Well, I've taken care of that now, and I'll move on with my life . . .' But I had so many people that were writing me . . . and asking me . . . 'How did you do it?' There were people in need of help, and at that point I realized there was a big need for help with people in a treatment center."*[4]

*"Betty Ford made the role of First Lady a contemporary and realistic sort of position," notes historian Carl Anthony. "She humanized it."*[5] *In 1982 she lent her name to a clinic for which she had served as fundraiser. Alan Leshner, director of the National Institute on Drug Abuse, comments, "She helped destigmatize addiction by, in effect, saying 'This could happen to anyone.'"*[6] *Mrs. Ford continues to play an active role in her clinic, beyond fundraising. She welcomes patients, sometimes with an embrace and a few comforting words. As she says, "[A]nything with my name on it, I'm going to be there to see that it goes along the way I feel is the most efficient and the best."*[7]

*Today, a generation later, talk of illness and personal issues is much more common. And while many people may feel that they don't want to listen to one more celebrity discuss a personal problem, it is well to note that far greater good has emerged. And for that we can thank women like Betty Ford; she kicked open the door to her own life, and in the process made millions of people think that they should be screened for cancer or that it was acceptable to seek treatment for addiction. For that, Betty Ford deserves recognition as a woman of courage, a person who was not afraid to speak out, even at the cost of her own privacy. Millions of people are alive today, or are living more healthful lives, because of her example.*

☙ ❧

Many times, when employees are asked in exit interviews why they are leaving, they say that their boss seldom, if ever, expressed any appreciation for their work. When interviewers follow up with the boss, the response that is often given is, "I didn't think it mattered." Fred Rogers showed in his daily television program how people mattered; he focused on children, and in doing so educated all of us about how much each of us matters to others. Betty Ford shared her personal afflictions as a means of showing that each of us matters as a human being. She has devoted much of her life to making things better one person at a time.

"In the twenty years I have been consulting," states Catherine Meeks, president of Meek Associates, summarizing her findings from thousands of employee interviews, "if I had to pick one thing that comes through to me loud and clear it's that organizations do a lousy job of recognizing people's contributions." According to motivational expert and author Bob Nelson, Meeks quotes employees as saying, "If my boss would just say thank you, if he would just acknowledge that I exist." She sums up her comments with the all-too-common complaint, "The only time I hear anything is when I screw up. I never hear when I do a good job."[8]

## A MATTER OF RECOGNITION

Well, it does matter. It matters a great deal. As mentioned earlier, employees have a strong desire for recognition. Surveys often show that recognition is a key motivator; sometimes, apart from salary, it is the chief reason why people work. It is human nature to want to be recognized. One person who studies workplace motivators is Dr. Gerald Graham, a professor of management at Wichita State University. One of his studies, which he shared with Bob Nelson, showed that three of the top five incentives that employees mention are free. These are (1) "a personal thank-you" from the boss, (2) a "written thank-you" from the same, and (3) "public praise."[9]

Yet recognition is one of the most overlooked incentives in the workplace. I believe most managers simply ignore the recognition factor for one of several reasons. First, they believe that recognizing one person means that they think that person is "better than" anyone else. Second, they think that recognition will make the person develop a "big head" and think he is better than everyone else. Third, they feel that they do not have time to "waste" on silly stuff like recognition.

Let's take these assumptions one at a time. First, recognizing a person's contribution is not an indication that you think that person is better than anyone else; it means that you think this person's performance is deserving of mention. A way to avoid this mistake is to ensure that everyone has an equal opportunity to succeed and to make it clear that you want your employees to be recognized. Second, recognizing a person's contribution will not in itself make her feel superior, but it will make her feel that she delivered a superior performance. Frankly, you want everyone to feel pride in her work. Some sales organizations want their people to have a sense of swagger about them because it means that they feel good about the company they represent, the products they sell, and the sales performance they deliver. Third, overlooking the need for recognition is plain stupid as well as shortsighted. A pat on the back or a word of praise in front of one's peers will do wonders for performance; it will encourage the person to keep on contributing, and all because you took a moment to recognize him.

Recognition is a leadership behavior and a prime driver of motivation. Mary Kay Ash created a network of self-employed people selling her line of cosmetics. The glue that held the organization together was recognition. Sales consultants wanted to achieve and be recognized, even if the reward was only a pin or a silver cup. What mattered was the recognition that they had done something special. Likewise at Zingerman's, under the direction of Ari Weinzweig and Paul Saginaw, the culture supports recognition on merit. Employees are provided with incentives for passing competency tests as well as opportunities to move up through the managerial ranks. If people know that they will be recognized for what they do, they will want to contribute as long as the forms of recognition are meaningful. Here are some things you can consider:

- *Do* not *treat everyone equally.* One of the mistakes that managers make is to feel that they should treat everyone equally. This is a fallacy. According to *First, Break All the Rules*, which was based upon a Gallup study of more than 80,000 managers, the most successful managers are those who devote a majority of their time to the high performers in their department.[10] Managers must treat all of their employees fairly and equitably, but devoting time and resources to the high-potential people is wise. Consider it your 80/20 rule. By spending time with those who achieve, the top 20 percent, you ensure success for your team and your department. You also enable those achievers to achieve even more. And if you provide an opportunity for the other 80 percent, you will have done what you can to encourage success at every level. (Do not confuse this 80/20 rule with forced ranking, which calls for mandatory placement of individuals into categories for appraisal and compensation purposes. This 80/20 rule is based upon practical experience, not arbitrarily imposed standards.)

- *Adopt a recognition mindset.* Organizations that perform well are organizations that recognize their contributors, i.e., the people who get things done the right way. The leaders of these organizations affirm the dignity of their people through their public statements as well as their private behaviors. They place an emphasis on training and development, and they recognize people who are well trained and capable. Managers in these organizations go out of their way to thank people for their contributions. They make it known that their people are an asset, not a cost.

- *Develop merit awards.* Part of treating everyone fairly and equitably is giving everyone an opportunity to be recognized. You want to enable people to be recognized for what they do. Sales-driven organizations are adept at creating tiered awards for sales quotas. More and more, however, as sales becomes more consultative and relies upon the integration of other functions like finance, logistics, and customer service, awards are not based strictly on quotas; there are awards for things like operational and service efficiencies.

- *Make the awards meaningful.* Recognition must be prompt and timely. Do not wait to recognize someone for a good effort. Even when people are striving to achieve monthly quotas, if they have a good week, let them know that you appreciate it. Give them a public pat on the back. At the same time, reward people the way they want to be rewarded. Many organizations are structured to give bonuses to salespeople. This is terrific, but do not forget the contributions of support functions. They have contributed too and may be deserving of a merit award. While bonuses are good, there are many more ways to recognize people, from public praise to incentive trips and merchandise. If you give these forms of recognition with meaning, people will be appreciative and will want to continue to achieve. If you give them out willy-nilly or to everyone, or if someone's entire pay is an incentive (e.g., car salespeople), you will burn people out and get mediocre performances over time.

- *Create heroes in the workplace.* Many people work very hard for their organizations. They make personal sacrifices in terms of time and commitment. This type of commitment needs to be recognized along with achievements. The concept of heroes in the workplace is gaining momentum. For example, at the annual sales meeting, develop a series of stories of sales excellence. You can do the same kind of video tribute to designers, engineers, and researchers. Customer service people can be lauded by their customers, often on video. Post the videos on the corporate Web site along with a story. At the same time you can laud heroes in many other ways: with e-mails, Web photos, bulletin board notices, and even a banner in the lunchroom. Some organizations do a good job of lauding people who develop best practices. Facilities and operations employees at the University of Michigan have a long history of developing best practices and disseminating them throughout the workplace. The developers of those best practices are cited in the newsletter as well as online and in town hall–style meetings.

- *Create a culture of recognition.* When you recognize people for their efforts and results, you are saying, "You are important, and we thank you." When you do this every day, week in and week out, you develop the habit of saying nice things to people. Pretty soon it is part of the culture. Southwest Airlines is famous for its commitment to recognition. Employees expect it and work to earn it. And the results are visible to customers: The employees are positive, upbeat, and friendly. Contrast that attitude with the anxiety and even surliness you encounter at other airlines. Recognizing people is more than something that's nice to do; it's something that's better to do because when people feel recognized, they feel wanted, and they want to do their best. When you put all of these recognition drivers together, you create a workplace where people want to contribute and be recognized. This is motivation at its most basic level, and it really works.

## NEED FOR AFFIRMATION

Recognition is essential if motivation is to occur. However, recognition does not always have to be about good performance. Sometimes recognition can be nothing more than an affirmation. Actor Sidney Poitier tells a poignant tale about trying to become an actor. At his first audition, he was unceremoniously ushered out of the room with the admonition never to return. The experience made Poitier realize that if he wanted to become an actor, he had better learn his craft. This began with a cram course in reading. One day an elderly Jewish waiter noticed Poitier reading in his restaurant. He befriended Poitier and became his tutor. What this kind man did for Poitier was a form of affirmation; he believed in him, not as a future actor or movie star, but simply as a person.[11]

Affirmation by another person is a powerful motivator, and it can easily be put into practice. Employees who work in organizations that have a culture of recognition will tell stories about the time they met the CEO. Invariably they will say that the leader was a "regular guy" and was very friendly. What that leader had done, as all good leaders do, was relate to the employee on a human level; he connected with the employee by asking questions, listening to what the employee had to say, and thanking the employee for his hard work. As a result, the employee felt 10 feet tall, and all because the CEO took a moment to have a conversation with him. Every manager can learn from such an example and spend a moment or two with her employees as a form of recognition of their efforts.

Affirmation is especially critical in tough times. When the organization is facing increased competition or a hostile takeover or an internal crisis involving reorganization, managers need to provide as much affirmation as possible. This can be difficult, since the managers themselves are as much victims of the upheaval as their employees are. But as managers they are responsible for their people; they need to do what they can to reach out and provide some kind of reassurance. For example, during a merger, information is scarce, chiefly for legal reasons. The rules of transparency that normally apply are replaced with opacity; managers are forbidden from disclosing what little information they have. But what managers can do is keep people informed and share what information they can. Affirmation then becomes paramount, letting people know that you value their performance. It is not a panacea, but a few words of encouragement can help ease very trying times. Senator John McCain tells a story of a low point in his 5½-year incarceration as a POW in North Vietnam. Interred in the "Hanoi Hilton" during Christmas of 1969, McCain was feeling pretty low, especially after hearing some Christmas carols over the camp intercom. Then he received a message, tapped in code through the walls of his cell, from a prisoner in the next cell: "We'll all be home for Christmas. God bless America."[12] It was just what McCain needed to hear at that moment. It was an affirmation from a fellow prisoner, who, sadly, never made it home himself, but who did what he could for others. Few of us will ever face that kind of deprivation, but all of us need moments of recognition by others.

## THE POWER WITHIN

Recognition drives motivation because it gives people a reason to believe in themselves. When managers recognize their people, they are really saying, "What you do matters to us." That sentiment goes to the fabric of our being and acts like a tonic to rejuvenate our spirits. It adds spring to the soles of our feel and zing to our spirit. And sometimes this feeling propels us with the kind of energy we need to push through a tough time, deal with a crisis, or finish a tough project. Recognition is a powerful force, so use it wisely.

## Insights into Motivation: Victor Vroom

Victor Vroom, an organizational theorist, developed a motivational theory based on expectancy, that is, what an individual gets in return for effort. Motivation, according to Vroom, is the result of three factors: expectancy, instrumentality, and valence. Expectancy is the outcome of performance; e.g., if I put in the effort, I will produce something. Instrumentality refers to the positive or negative consequences of the effort; e.g., I may get promoted, but on the other hand, my colleagues may resent my effort. Valence refers to the "value" an individual places on the "outcome"; e.g., I work hard, and I enjoy the perks. According to Vroom, variances in each of these factors affect motivation; e.g., good pay, hard work, and a strong work ethic result in a motivated employee. Likewise, low pay, hard work, and lack of will to work create a demotivated employee. It is important to note that two of Vroom's three factors (expectancy and valence) are intrinsic; the third factor (instrumentality) is extrinsic. In other words, the individual has control over what he will do and how he values it, but it is up to the employer to provide an adequate reward, or compensation. Expectancy theory lies at the heart of many incentive and bonus systems: Work hard, and you will be rewarded.[13]

## Motivation Planner: Recognize

Recognition lies at the heart and soul of motivation. All of us crave to be noticed for what we do. Use the following questions to help you discover ways in which you can recognize your people for their good work.

1. What percentage of your day do you spend supporting your top performers? What percentage of your time do you spend working with chronic underperformers? If you spend more time with chronic underperformers, what can you do to reverse the equation and spend more time (and resources) with top performers?

2. How can you develop a recognition program in your workplace? Whom do you have to talk to? How will you broach the topic with your people?

3. What kind of merit awards (e.g., length of service, improved quality, improved customer service) would be significant to your people?

4. How can you reward people in ways that are meaningful to them (and affordable by your organization)?

5. Think about the people in your organization who are doing great work. How can you publicize their efforts? What would you accomplish by recognizing them as "heroes"?

6. How can you foster a culture of recognition? How do you persuade your boss of the benefits of such a culture?

7. How do you demonstrate affirmation in your workplace? How do you make it known that you value the contributions of your people?

## MARY KAY ASH

She recalled standing in line for three hours when she was a young woman to shake the hand of a corporate bigwig as part of a recognition ceremony. When her turn finally came, her sense of anticipation was immediately dashed by the executive's behavior: He took her hand, but he looked right past her to see how many other women were still standing in line. Right then and there she resolved that if anyone ever stood in line to shake her hand, she would look that person in the eye and acknowledge her presence. As she writes, "It's always important to focus all of your attention on the person in front of you." She was Mary Kay Ash, founder and CEO of Mary Kay Cosmetics, and that statement gets to the heart of who she was as an entrepreneur, a person, and a supreme motivator.[14]

Building a business, especially building one from scratch, requires vision, courage, gumption, and, most of all, people. And when you are in the direct sales business, your relationships with your employees and your customers will make or break the enterprise. Mary Kay, Inc. (successor to Mary Kay Cosmetics), is built on three principles: the Golden Rule, the troika of God-family-career (in that order), and the "potential of people."[15] The underlying theme that links all three principles is unwavering faith in doing what is right in order to do well. That concept led Mary Kay to create a multibillion-dollar business that is wholly people-centric. Most of the people who work for Mary Kay are independent contractors; therefore, they need a strong sense of motivation in order to do what they do. Mary Kay was able to tap into their need by sharing her own success. As a result, her story is one from which all of us can learn.

## "YOU CAN DO IT!"

Something of a precocious child, Mary Kay was born in Hot Wells, Texas, in 1918; she was the youngest of three children and the only one who was still at home when her father contracted tuberculosis and became an invalid. Her mother, whom Mary Kay credits as her tower of strength, had to go to work, leaving Mary Kay, beginning at age seven, to cook and clean for her father, as well as attend school. And Mary Kay did so with an amazing sense of competence, coupled with an indomitable sense of self that was in part nurtured by her mother, who always reminded her, when she was cooking or doing anything else, "You can do it, honey!"[16] That phrase, "You can do it!" became a mantra for the young Mary Kay as well as the entrepreneurial Mary Kay.

She married at 17 and had three children by the outbreak of World War II, in which her husband served. At the end of the war, he asked for a divorce. It was an experience that shattered her confidence, but one that spurred her in the only direction she ever went: forward.[17] Having dabbled in sales, she pursued it full time, working for Stanley Home Products, among other companies. It was as a saleswoman and later as a sales trainer and a de facto manager that she learned the trade and also gained insights into what makes people want to buy and what makes people want to achieve. In fact, upon her retirement from a career working for others, she set out to write a book about how a company should be run. The book would have to wait; putting ideas down on paper spurred her to think about starting her own company.[18]

## "DREAM COMPANY"

Part of her thinking about her "dream company" came from the negative experiences she had had as a woman. She writes in her autobiography, *Miracles Happen*, that as a sales trainer, she trained managers who would soon be her boss. She submitted marketing plans but was dismissed by her bosses, who said, "Mary Kay, you're thinking just like a woman." Her compensation was notably less than that of her male counterparts; when she complained, her bosses reminded her that men "had families to support." As if Mary Kay, a mother of three, did not have such responsibilities. Women a generation later would tear down this kind of behavior irrevocably. But Mary Kay was way out front; she started her business in 1963 with an idea: "Everyone Welcome—Especially Women."[19]

At the heart of Mary Kay's success was her ability to sell. Good salespeople like being with people, talking to them, and offering them something new and different. Good salespeople are expert at reading people; they combine an ability to discern clues to interest or disinterest with a knowledge of basic human wants and needs. Good salespeople, in short, understand what makes people tick. In this Mary Kay was among the very best. Her gift was her ability to take what she knew about selling products to people and apply it to selling ideas to people. Mary Kay Cosmetics was her business; her idea was to enable women to achieve their own goals by controlling their own financial destiny. In this, Mary Kay was years ahead of her time.

Rather than simply talk up her vision, which she did frequently, she made it real. First, she created a direct sales business where women bought and sold her cosmetics. Second, she provided these women with training that enabled them to teach the secrets of personal grooming and beauty to their customers. Third, she gave women a strategy for success; she taught people to prioritize, and she made career paths clear and accessible. And fourth (and perhaps this is her genius), she recognized her people for doing what they did well—selling.

## CULTURE OF RECOGNITION

The heart of Mary Kay, which later became the heart of Mary Kay, Inc., is recognition, taking note of the person in front of you. She writes of the "philosophy of praising" at her company. Through praise, or acknowledging people for a job well done, the company affirms a beauty consultant's (Mary Kay–ese for salesperson) self-worth, which in turn leads her to develop a better sense of self and become a more confident, as well as ambitious, salesperson. Mary Kay developed something she called the Ladder of Success; it is an incentive-based goal strategy in which people compete against themselves and their peers. Incentives are nothing new in sales. What Mary Kay did was make them inclusive; every Mary Kay consultant can compete. In addition, the goals are explicit. Sales consultants know exactly what they have to do to move up the ladder. Inclusion and explicitness are central conditions for motivation; by tapping into both, Mary Kay put teeth into the "philosophy of praise."[20]

The rewards at Mary Kay, Inc., are real. The highest achievers can earn points toward winning a pink Cadillac. It was an incentive of which Mary Kay said, "It got the attention our top producers deserved." The attention was not only internal; the general public, and with it legions of customers and potential employees, also noticed. Mary Kay also offered other GM cars in pink, escalating in status with the achievement of sales goals.[21] The Ladder of Success also includes a host of other incentives, some as simple as a loving cup. What's important to note is that incentives start at very low levels; for example, a beauty consultant might get a ribbon for conducting a beauty class; stars are awarded for recruits; and diamond rings are given for the achievement of high sales goals. While it is nice to receive a gift, the real reward is not the gift itself; it is the affirmation of success. And in sales, as in life, success breeds success.[22]

The annual conference, known as the Seminar, is the most affirming group event on the calendar. What began as a three-day event in the 1960s has grown to become a month-long event encompassing successive waves of sales consultants, some 50,000 in all. Salespeople converge on the event for a few days of celebrating their success, basking in the affirmative culture of Mary Kay, and listening to the company's senior leaders extol the contributions of the sales force. For people who work in direct sales organizations, this coming together is a big event; it becomes an opportunity to share success stories, learn new techniques, and get up to speed on the product line. There is also live entertainment, which the company refers to as its own "Academy Awards."[23]

Mary Kay was someone who strove for personal connections, as all good salespeople do. Stories of her reaching out and touching the lives of her people are legion within Mary Kay Cosmetics. Likewise, she was moved by the impact she had on people's lives. She liked to tell stories of the many women who had risen through the ranks and thereby improved the lot of their families, in some instances enabling their husbands to quit their jobs to pursue "dream jobs" of their own. Collections of such stories, referred to as "I-stories," are contained in a Mary Kay publication, *Room at the Top*. Publishing stories such as these not only provides recognition to the storyteller, but gives the people reading them the hope that they too can succeed.[24]

## INSIDE OUT

Genuine motivation comes from within. Mary Kay is no exception. When she describes her childhood, she speaks of an inner drive to do better. As a young salesperson, she strove for recognition; she wanted to be "Miss Dallas," the highest-achieving saleswoman in her territory. Such drive was inherent in her persona, but it was nurtured by hard circumstances. As a child, she cared for her father. She was divorced and left with three young children. As she was about to start her company, her second husband suffered a fatal heart attack. As painful as these events were, she had the drive and the will to overcome adversity. Her motivation was internal.[25]

And as a businesswoman she strove to institutionalize her drive. She communicated her philosophy at corporate gatherings, at public events, and through her writings. Her book *Mary Kay on People Management* was a best-seller for years and was used at the Harvard Business School. Passion for people and enthusiasm for her work were essential to Mary Kay. As she wrote in *Miracles Happen*, "Even after all these years in business, no matter how exhausted I may be the night before, I awaken each morning with renewed enthusiasm. I love what I do, and each day presents new opportunities to love and encourage each working woman to succeed."[26]

## FAMILY COMMITMENT

Family was important to Mary Kay; she employed all three of her children in the business. Her son Richard Rogers helped her start the business and served as CEO. As a woman, she knew the discrimination that women suffered because of familial obligations, so in her company she insisted on family (second only to God) coming before career. When her third husband, Mel, was ill, she took time off from the business to be with him. What we today call "work/life integration" was one of her founding principles, beginning in 1963 with the start of the company.[27] Mary Kay did not just "talk the talk, she walked it." She spent countless hours writing birthday notes to her employees as well as sympathy cards to those who had lost loved ones.[28]

Mary Kay considered herself a committed Christian. With "God as her partner," Mary Kay hewed to high ethical standards because she believed "that what you *did* was more important than what you *said*." She lived this commitment daily in her commitment to her people, but she was pragmatic, too. "I'm careful to remember that we are a business and that I must avoid preaching to our people." She acknowledged the religious diversity of her associates, noting that many of them did seem to be "spiritually strong people." Mary Kay also was generous in giving her time as well as her wealth to church and charity; today the Mary Kay Charitable Foundation, established in 1996, stands testament to her philanthropy.[29]

## LASTING IMPRESSION

Reading her works today, it is tempting to be patronizing; after all, Mary Kay writes in cheery prose that is relentlessly upbeat, focused on the positive, and grounded in her faith in God and her people. And then there is the pink, the hallmark color of her company. But it's good to recall that she has written that "at the time we began our company, *pink was not my favorite color!*" Pink was chosen because it would stand out in a white bathroom.[30] The point is that Mary Kay was a shrewd businesswoman, but, more importantly, she ran her business by treating her employees the way she would have liked to have been treated herself—as a smart, capable businesswoman. And she gave back to the business by investing herself in the reward and recognition process.

A measure of an entrepreneur's success is what happens after the founder leaves. Mary Kay suffered a stroke in 1996, ending her "day to day involvement in the firm." Her presence was missed, and the company experienced some "missteps," which management freely admits. However, in June 2001, her son Richard Rogers returned to the helm as chairman and returned the company to what is referred to as the "Mary Kay Way." By that, Rogers and his management team meant a return to the values of the founder and a renewed commitment to the culture she had created.[31]

Upon Mary Kay's death in 2001, accolades poured in from all over the world. Her own hometown paper summed it up best: "She was a classic steel magnolia. Tough-minded and tender-hearted, proudly feminine to her Texas core."[32] John P. Kotter, a noted leadership author and Harvard Business School professor, said, "She was an extraordinary business leader in an age when far too many people running corporations are competent managers, but nothing more." Kotter added, "She was also a great entrepreneur."[33] Perhaps Zig Ziglar, motivational author and speaker par excellence, best summed her up by saying, "Mary Kay was the wholesome personification of the American dream. . . . She was a very wise lady. She was a people person. She was very sensitive to the importance of recognizing people."[34] People were central to Mary Kay's mission in life, and it was a mission that involved elevating others to feel good about themselves as women, as professionals, and as human beings.

## Lessons in Leadership Motivation

- *You can do it!* Mary Kay's mother taught her that she could do anything she put her mind to. This was a philosophy that Mary Kay used to overcome personal adversity and business challenges.
- *Recognize achievement.* Mary Kay practiced the "philosophy of praise." She wanted people to know that their contributions were appreciated, and her company awarded incentives to affirm that.
- *Make people feel important.* People were important to Mary Kay. She invested her time in getting to know her associates and personally thanking them for their efforts.
- *Share the love.* Mary Kay created the annual Seminar as a way for her associates to get together to share their stories and to be recognized.
- *Live the values.* Mary Kay, Inc., runs on three principles: God, family, and career. She practiced these principles in her own life and insisted that the people in her organization do the same.

# Exhort

- *Sacrifice*
- *Inspire*

**M**otivation requires exhortation, the rallying of others to the cause. Leaders must be seen, heard, and felt. When they are, people experience their leaders, and they do this most keenly when they see their leaders sacrifice by putting the needs of others first. Experiencing leadership is a form of inspiration, something that derives from the process of exhortation, bringing people together for an honorable purpose.

C H A P T E R 8

"We do not want your civilization. We would live as
our fathers did, and their fathers before them!"

*Crazy Horse (attributed)*
*Sioux warrior*

# SACRIFICE

## HEROES FOR OUR TIME

*S*ADLY, IN THIS ERA THAT SOME CALL AN AGE OF IRONY, *when so
much of what we perceive is supposed to be tongue in
cheek, what truly grabs us is not an ironic smile, but rather
an ironic punch in the gut. Such was the case with the deaths of
two men of peace, both of whom died in very different circumstances, but both of whom were committed to their causes.*

*The first is Dr. David Applebaum, an emergency room
physician working in Jerusalem. He was a victim of what he*

*had tried so hard in his practice to ameliorate the suffering from—a suicide bombing. He was out with his daughter, Nava, on the eve of her wedding, and both were killed by a Palestinian suicide bomber who detonated himself in the street where they were standing. Fifteen Israelis lost their lives in terrorist bombings on that day. Applebaum's colleagues in the Israeli rescue service, in which he had served for two decades, identified his body.*

*A native of Cleveland, Applebaum was both a man of the cloth and a man of science. Ordained as a rabbi in 1974, he graduated from the Medical College of Ohio in Toledo in 1978. After emigrating to Israel in the early eighties, he did some pioneering work on thrombolysis, the process of dissolving blood clots in heart attack victims. He also opened clinics as an alternative to hospital emergency rooms. He never lost his touch with patient care. He installed a computer system in the waiting room in the hospital emergency room that he managed in order to cut patient wait times. His colleagues noted that Dr. Applebaum arrived early and stayed late: "He always stayed until the last patient had been assessed and treated."*

*Dr. David Applebaum was a man of deep faith. He tutored his son in the Torah every Wednesday at his son's seminary school. He was a passionate student himself as a boy, yet in an era in which faith has made many people oblivious to the virtues of other faiths, it did just the opposite for Dr. Applebaum. It opened him to the humanity of all. In an interview in the aftermath of a bombing in which many children had died, he said, "One of our very important tasks is to unite the children with their parents. We know the separation in these incidents causes intense worry and fear." It is little wonder, then, that one colleague said of him after his death, "He commanded respect and authority, but not in a threatening way. He always had a smile."*

*If a man working amidst the horror of daily bombings that maim and kill, not to mention make an entire populace feel as if it is standing at the edge of a metaphorical precipice, can remain calm and radiate warmth and sincerity, then the least we can do is honor the memory of Dr. David Applebaum as one of hope and inspiration.*[1]

*The second example is Sergio Vieira de Mello, a Brazilian-born U.N. diplomat. Although he prided himself on being a diplomat who "liked to get his boots dirty from time to time," he did not believe that the presence of the United Nations in a war that it did not sanction was proper. But when Kofi Annan, secretary general as well as his mentor and boss, said, "I want you to go to Baghdad to be my little Nelson Mandela," Vieira de Mello did his duty.*

*The son of a Brazilian ambassador, Vieira de Mello was educated at the Sorbonne. Handsome, urbane, and at home with people from many cultures, Vieira de Mello was a worldly man, but also a man who understood that diplomats do not work in ivory towers; they must wallow in the blood and the muck as well. And he did plenty of the latter.*

*A glance at his résumé shows his resolve to be in the thick of it: Bangladesh, Cyprus, Lebanon, and Peru, all of which were going through a war or civil war when he was there. He also helped with mine-clearing efforts in Cambodia. Most recently he had served in Kosovo and East Timor. In short, for a man who was at home in the salons of Europe and the diplomatic hallways of foreign capitals, Sergio Vieira de Mello had a capacity for hard work in the trenches. And he was rewarded for his service by being named U.N. high commissioner for human rights.*

*He took a leave from that post to serve in Iraq. Ironically, he told a reporter for the Brazilian daily* O Estado de São Paulo, *"I don't feel in danger as I did in other places where I was working for the UN. I don't feel a climate of hostility." And he demonstrated keen sympathy for the Iraqis. "This must be one of the most humiliating periods in history for [them]. Who would like their country to be occupied? I would not like to see foreign tanks in Copacabana [a beach in Rio de Janeiro]." A short time later, on August 19, 2003, Vieira de Mello was working in the U.N.'s Baghdad headquarters when a suicide bomber drove into the building, taking it down and killing more than 20 people, many of*

*them U.N. diplomats like himself. "I can think of no one we could*
*less afford to spare," said a disconsolate Kofi Annan.*

*"All that is necessary for evil to triumph,"* The Economist
*noted, quoting Edmund Burke, in its obituary of Vieira de Mello,*
*"is for good men to do nothing." Sergio Vieira de Mello devoted*
*his life to peace and nation building, and he gave his life for it.*[2]

*It is from the heroic example of others that we draw our*
*greatest lessons, lessons that last for generations. The sacrifices*
*of men like Dr. David Applebaum and Sergio de Vieira de Mello*
*remind us of how much more work we have to do.*

*Sacrifice* is a word that is not often heard in management circles.
Sometimes the word is invoked by managers who are asking
employees (but not themselves, thank you) to forgo a pay raise to
help the company weather hard times. And the word was much
heard in the early 2000s among employees and shareholders who
watched their 401(k) funds dwindle. But it is not a word that you
hear managers apply to themselves. Let's be honest. Many managers are overworked; they put in long hours every week and
often log time on the weekends. They are taking time away from
their families and their personal pursuits. Their sacrifice takes a
toll on body, mind, and spirit. They lose focus, enthusiasm, and
sense of purpose. They become demotivated and burned out.
This is certainly a sacrifice, but it is not the kind that anyone
should seek to emulate. The kind of sacrifice that matters most is
the kind that improves the lives of others. David Applebaum and
Sergio Vieira de Mello put themselves in the line of fire as a
means of making life better for individuals, as Dr. Applebaum
did, and for nations, as Commissioner Vieira de Mello did. Both
were heroes in the service of humanity.

## HEROIC SACRIFICE

The kind of sacrifice required if motivation is to occur is the kind
of sacrifice that involves the setting aside of self for the good of

others. The military has a rich tradition of sacrifice. This sacrifice begins with the oath of allegiance; from that moment onward, the soldier pledges himself to duty, honor, and country. When our government sends soldiers into combat, they make a sacrifice to be there, and some of them never return, making the ultimate sacrifice for their country. Soldiers who experience such sacrifice understand what it means to endure the deprivations of living outside for months on end, eating unappetizing food meal after meal, being away from home, and, worst of all, seeing fellow soldiers fall. Captain Lionel Ferguson of the British Army, who fought at the Battle of the Somme, penned the following words a few years after the Armistice that ended World War I:

> To those in years to come [who] may ever read these notes: please remember, none of us regret our experiences; but we have had our bad times. We have formed never to be forgotten friendships . . . but for the first time in our lives we have known the meaning of "Hunger," "Thirst," "Dirt," "Death" and other privations. We, I think, have all known the meaning of "Fear" as we have never seen it. . . . Now, some years later, we who went through it, know that those at home never did realize the work that "The Solider" was asked to do. Those who talk of the "The Next War" are people who never "suffered" in a front-line trench; for never, never again will those who have come back, advocate another War.[3]

You can discern in Captain Ferguson's words—and in the millions of other letters that soldiers in every war have written—the value of sacrifice, but also the terrible cost it exacts. Likewise, police officers and firefighters routinely make sacrifices in the interest of serving and protecting our communities. All too often we read stories of police officers killed in the line of duty or firefighters perishing in a burning building trying to make a rescue. Wiser men may walk away, but those who serve their country and their community cannot. The core of their service lies in sacrifice. Their stories of heroism (and they would be the last to consider themselves heroes) motivate others to take their place and to serve as bravely and honorably as they did. Crazy Horse was someone who put his own needs second. Designated as a special provider for his tribe, he shared his hunts with the women and children first. He also lived humbly, without the trappings that other great warriors were entitled to display.

Entrepreneurs seldom make the kind of sacrifice that puts their lives in peril, but they do sacrifice mightily to get their businesses off the ground. Henry Ford failed twice as an entrepreneur before he launched Ford Motor Company. Ray Kroc never made a dime from the McDonald's franchise for the first 10 years of its operation. He insisted that the operators and employees be paid before he was.

## BUILDING THE ORGANIZATION THE HARD WAY

Leaders must put the needs of the organization first. When they do, people can see that the leader is acting for the good of the organization. This builds trust, which will help the leader gain support for tough decisions and gain momentum for initiatives. Also, if the leader actively promotes other people and other people's ideas, she will be seen as someone who walks the talk when it comes to putting people first. This action is a great motivator in itself. Here are some ways to make sacrifice a positive force in the organization.

- *Put other people first.* The essence of sacrifice is giving up something for someone else. Before you can sacrifice, you had better know the people for whom you are sacrificing. That attitude begins with an attitude of service to others. Robert Greenleaf, a sociologist and philosopher, advocated a concept, derived from the Judeo-Christian ethos of service to others, that he called servant leadership. He wrote that leaders need to serve their people. This form of service begins with understanding who they are as people and then trying to run the organization in such a way that it fulfills their needs. Servant leaders can be businesspeople.

Max de Pree, the author and former CEO, is a strong pro-
ponent of servant leadership and made it a hallmark of his
tenure at Herman Miller, the office furniture maker. You
will still have to make tough decisions, but you will do it
with the rights of employees as well as customers in mind.
For example, you spend time and money developing people, and you devote resources to designing and delivering
quality products. You also commit to the community. A
concept that is complementary to servant leadership is sustainability, meaning a commitment to the triple bottom
line: making a business fiscally, socially, and environmen-
tally accountable. A servant leader who puts people first
will certainly strive for sustainability.

- *Pick the right moment.* Sacrifices, like crises, are not
  events that can be scheduled. Crises, however, do create
  opportunities for sacrifice. For example, when there is an
  accident at a plant or a shooting in an office building, the
  leaders of the organization need to be present and available
  to the victims. As mayor of New York City, Rudy Giuliani
  was famous for always making time to attend the funerals
  of city workers, most often police officers and firefighters,
  who died in the line of duty. Giuliani's attendance demonstrated that the city cared about its employees and stood by
  their families. You don't have to wait for a tragedy to
  occur. During stressful times—when the company is facing competitive pressures, a merger is pending, or some
  other event that makes all employees uneasy is taking
  place—leaders again need to be front and center. They
  need to pitch in and be available to let people know that
  they care about them.

- *Be the first to sacrifice.* Sacrifice for others is an act of
  leadership; it is an act that puts others first. Ernest Shackleton shared his food with those who were ill. Leaders
  need to be the ones setting the example. When times are
  tough, the CEO should be the first to surrender the pay

raise. When times are good, the CEO should be sending out the bonus checks and thanking people for their contributions, especially if they have forgone raises during bad times. When people see their leaders putting themselves on the line, they will take notice. Example speaks far more eloquently than words do.

- *Recognize the sacrifices of others.* When people make an effort for others, giving of themselves to others, recognize that act. In the previous chapter, we discussed recognition of contributions. The same holds for sacrifice. The reason that the U.S. Marine Corps has such high esprit de corps is that those on active duty are aware of the sacrifices of those who came before. Marines today know all about past battles; they know the Medal of Honor winners, those whose valor was recognized by Congress by being given the highest award any soldier can receive. They also know that to become a Marine requires sacrifice; you have to work hard to get through basic training and to qualify for active service. In the civilian sector, social service agencies that benefit from philanthropy do a good job of recognizing the contributions of their donor base.

## QUESTION THE VALUE OF SACRIFICE

As noble as the notion of sacrifice is, it must be questioned from time to time. John F. Kennedy wrote letters home from the South Pacific questioning the competency of some of the commanders he encountered and wondering if the kind of sacrifice he and his men were making were necessary.[4] A generation later, Senator John Kerry, a decorated Navy patrol boat captain, questioned the sacrifices that the men of his generation were making in South Vietnam. While Kennedy was certain that the war against Japan was noble, Kerry became more and more convinced that U.S. involvement in Vietnam was not.[5] Both were honorable men and patriots to the core; their questioning was a product of the American value system and the freedom that we have to question our government and criticize it when necessary.

Raising questions is all the more imperative in the corporate arena. While physical safety is not often the issue, the spending of resources (time, manpower, and capital) is. Every manager needs to question herself to make certain that the sacrifices she is making, or is asking her people to make, are adding value to the enterprise. For example, if you ask an employee to work overtime to help with a project that is significant to the company's future, that's a valid request. If you ask an employee to work overtime to help with clerical work that should have been done by others, but was not, the sacrifice may not be valid. It is a failure of management that allowed the clerical overload in the first place, and it should not fall to others to clean up the work through overtime. Sometimes, however, the manager may find herself staying late to do such work, and by doing so, she sets a positive example. Others may wish to join in, but they should not be asked to do so.

## THE GREATER THE CAUSE

When executed for a cause greater than the individual and for a gain greater than a single person, sacrifice is an act of nobility. As such, it has the power to catch the attention of others and cause them to consider the character and values of their leader. Some may be motivated to emulate the leader. For example, when employees see that their manager is willing to spend time with them, even sacrificing personal time to help them with a project or a process, they feel a sense of kinship that is real. They develop a sense of respect for the manager because they see that he is trying to do the right thing and putting others ahead of himself. This kind of sacrifice propagates itself and leads to the improved performance that is characteristic of a work environment in which people are motivated.

As a final thought on sacrifice, it is useful to recall the example of Abraham Lincoln at Gettysburg. In his 242-word address, he captured the heroic nature of sacrifice in service to a cause, preservation of the Union, and reiterated the honor of the sacrifices made by those who had fought and died there. Lincoln's words in November 1863, 18 months before war's end, also broached the concept of healing the wounds so that the Union, when preserved, could once again be one. In doing so, Lincoln made it clear that sacrifices had been made by both North and South, and that as a result it would require the joint participation of both to make the nation whole again. It is for this reason that the Gettysburg Address continues to resonate with us today.

## Insights into Motivation: Avoidance Theory

Some academic theories of motivation evolved from studies of what has become known as "avoidance theory." As it applies to the workplace, avoidance theory postulates that employees will, if given a choice, take the path of least resistance. Often the easy way is the best way, but in difficult times this may not be the case, and so it falls to the leader to persuade his followers to do something that is hard rather than what is easy. This is where motivation is critical. The leader must enable his people to see that doing what is hard will be better for them and the organization in the long run. That's easy to say, but challenging to implement, and it is what leaders in organizations face every day—resistance or avoidance.

## Motivation Planner: Sacrifice

Sacrifice is a commitment to others. When it is done for the right reasons, it builds esprit de corps and trust. Use the following questions to see how you might apply the lessons of sacrifice to your workplace.

1. How can you demonstrate that the people in your organization are a priority? How do you get beyond words to actions?

2. Consider the past year. When would have been a good time for you to "take one for the team," e.g., make a sacrifice for the good of others? Did you do it? Why or why not? What will you do differently next time?

3. How can you let people know that you are willing to be the first to "take one for the team"? What do you hope others will learn from your attitude?

4. When other people put the needs of others first (i.e., sacrifice), how do you let them know that you appreciate (recognize) their effort?

5. How will you know when a sacrifice is worth it? What criteria will you employ to make this decision? How will you know when you have made the right decision?

## CRAZY HORSE

It must have been one of the hardest, if not the hardest, thing he had ever had to do. For his entire adult life, he had been free to go where he wanted to go—all across the Great Plains to hunt for game or to challenge his enemies. But now he put himself second and the welfare of his people first. He was Crazy Horse, and he was about to lead a group of 900 people from his tribe into a camp supervised by the U.S. Army. For them, it would be the beginning of a new chapter of learning to live in "civilization." For Crazy Horse, it would be the beginning of the end. It was a moment of supreme sacrifice.[6]

Very few facts about the life and times of Crazy Horse are known. He lived his life among illiterate people, and except for the very end of his life, we have very little factual information about him. Much of what we know about his life is based upon the oral histories of his contemporaries, who were well into their dotage when they gave testimony. As is common among indigenous peoples, their focus was not on the written word, but on the spoken. And over the years the oral history changes as circumstances change to reflect the evolving conditions. Crazy Horse's contemporaries had reason to remember him as larger than life because he was one of the last of his kind, a genuine hero who lived as he chose to live with honor and dignity until he surrendered to a force greater than himself—the need to protect others. What cannot be disputed is the impact he had on his people then and the influence he brings today. And it is for that reason that Crazy Horse serves as a role model.[7]

## EARLY LIFE

A distinguishing characteristic of Crazy Horse was his solitary nature. Perhaps being the son of a medicine man led him to spend great amounts of time by himself as an adult. Crazy Horse viewed "animals as teachers." He learned the ways of the prairie and how to detect changes in the weather. His independent nature set him apart from his tribe in some ways, but the Sioux of his time, according to historians, seemed very tolerant of those who took divergent paths. In this sense, Crazy Horse seems more modern in his outlook than his contemporaries in white culture.[8]

In that culture, the highlight of a young man's life was choosing a name. Young braves would undergo elaborate preparations, including deprivations supervised by adult males, in order to provoke dreams that might indicate what they were supposed to do with their lives. Not Crazy Horse. He simply wandered off alone on his own sort of vision quest. He did have a dream, but, true to his independent streak, he did not share it with others for years. Crazy Horse's dream did predict his life course: He would become a great warrior, and he would be protected from his enemies if he took nothing for himself. He also was instructed to shun the trappings of war. In contrast to most chiefs, who wore elaborate war bonnets of eagle feathers, Crazy Horse wore a single eagle feather and little or no war paint; he also kept a pebble behind his ear. His dream also contained a warning: Harm would come to him from his own people. Whether this dream really occurred is beside the point; what is important is that Crazy Horse lived by a core principle that put others before himself.[9]

Communalism was common among Plains Indians, but Crazy Horse's selflessness was notable. He was made a Shirt Wearer; it was an honorific title but one of great responsibility because it made him a de facto provider for his people. He shared the bounty of buffalo and game hunts as well as ponies taken from other Indian tribes in battle. And, as was the custom, he was expected to "give away the choicest cuts such as the tongue or the hump of the buffalo, saving only the stringy leg muscle for himself." In other words, he put others first, even in small things.[10]

## VERSUS YELLOW HAIR

Native peoples have legends, but so, too, do non-natives. Crazy Horse is best known for defeating George Custer at the battle of Little Bighorn in June 1876. While Custer was defeated outright, it was really as a result of hubris rather than through the actions of a single warrior, especially one who was not a chief. There is no question but that Custer was itching for a fight and the Indians were preparing for one. Sitting Bull had rallied the Sioux and the Cheyenne to his cause; he had performed a Sun Dance, where pieces of his flesh were cut; and he had stared at the sun. Upon passing out, he had a vision of victory. As historian Stephen Ambrose tells us in *Crazy Horse and Custer*, this battle was one of the few times that the Sioux fought as one united force rather than as scattered bands, as they typically did in intertribal Indian warfare, where killing the enemy was not the purpose—stealing ponies and one-upmanship were more important.[11]

At the Little Bighorn, the stakes were higher. The Sioux were fighting for their way of life, a way of life that Red Cloud, among others, had already rejected and that other Sioux certainly sensed was doomed. Not Crazy Horse; he was an independent thinker as well as a communal protector. So when Custer, who had cut his flowing golden locks short, plunged into an area that the Indians called Creasy Grass, more than 3,000 Indian braves were waiting. How many participated in the battle is not known, but Larry McMurtry, in his book *Crazy Horse*, writes that "as many as two thousand horses may have been in motion during this battle; the dust they raised . . . would soon have become phantasmagoria; it would have been difficult for anyone to see well, or far."[12] Therefore, no one knows who killed Custer, but some historians, among them Ambrose, credit Crazy Horse with staging a brilliant flanking move that prevented Custer from taking the high ground, which today is known as Custer Hill. Such a move would have required great bravery because the Seventh Cavalry, while vastly outnumbered, was well armed and well trained to lay down heavy gunfire. As the afternoon waned, all 262 men of the Seventh Cavalry were dead, bringing down many Sioux with them.[13]

The victory was pyrrhic. Rather than driving the white man away, it only stiffened his resolve. A succession of military moves against the Plains Indians, including the Cheyenne, put an end to the Great Plains War. Within a year, the Sioux were either in agency camps or on the run. Sitting Bull, who had orchestrated the union of tribes in the summer of 1876, fled to Canada the following spring. He would later return, only to be killed by one of his own prior to the Battle of Wounded Knee in 1890. For Crazy Horse, though, the victory did two things: It elevated him to a heroic stature among his own people, and it made him a marked man to the Army.[14]

## BLACK BUFFALO WOMAN

Crazy Horse was not without his faults. He ran off with another man's wife, Black Buffalo Woman. Crazy Horse had courted Black Buffalo for years, but she had chosen to marry another brave, No Water. Over the years, Crazy Horse remained attentive to Black Buffalo, much to the irritation of No Water. The Sioux of the time did allow for what we would call divorce; women could chose other spouses, just as men could, but restitution had to be provided. In this instance, it was not; Crazy Horse and Black Buffalo simply eloped. They were caught within a day, and No Water actually pulled a pistol on Crazy Horse and shot him. Crazy Horse survived, but his dignity did not. He was forced to give up his position as a Shirt Wearer. Shirt or no shirt, however, Crazy Horse continued, as he had done throughout his adult life, to provide for his people. He even married, twice, and fathered children; a daughter, perhaps a product of his liaison with Black Buffalo, died in 1940.[15]

## LAST STAND

The winter of 1876–1877 was very hard on Crazy Horse's people. Cold and hungry, they wanted to join Red Cloud's camp, where in exchange for their freedom they would have food and shelter. Crazy Horse refused to allow anyone to surrender, and in fact even prevented those who did escape from getting very far by shooting their horses. As Stephen Ambrose says, "It was a very un-Indian-like thing for him to do, forcing people to stay with him in extreme danger." Ambrose speculates that Crazy Horse feared that his people would be executed if they surrendered.[16]

Whatever his motives had been in the winter, his hardness dissolved in the spring of 1877. After a parley with Red Cloud, Crazy Horse decided to bring his people in. His surrender certainly did not appear like one. Entering Camp Robinson, the fort adjacent to the Red Cloud Agency, Crazy Horse led a group of braves wearing war bonnets and riding their beloved ponies as the Indian women sang. Crazy Horse must have cut an impressive figure, with a Winchester slung across his lap and the solitary eagle feather in his headband. It was the last time Crazy Horse would ever hold such command, but his behavior inspired the young braves in the camp as well as earning the respect of the soldiers.[17]

The respect that Crazy Horse earned from the young and from his former enemies caused jealousy among the Sioux chiefs, namely Red Cloud and Spotted Tail. Red Cloud had never been a warrior chief, and Spotted Tail had been in camp for a long time. They spread false rumors to the officers and soldiers to the effect that Crazy Horse was plotting against them. While many in the Army respected Crazy Horse, they also feared him as they feared no other Indian. Even though Crazy Horse had given his word that he would fight no more, the intent of his words was not interpreted correctly. In the midst of this rumormongering, Crazy Horse escaped, but was later caught and was brought into the fort once again, this time into a jail cell. (General George Crook intended to ship him to Florida to a prison on the Dry Tortugas.) At the last moment, Crazy Horse broke free, but he was subdued, and, as his vision of many years before had predicted, while his arms were "held by his own people," he was bayoneted by a soldier and carried to a bed. Worm, Crazy Horse's father, was at his side and heard him say, "Father, it is no use to depend on me. I am going to die." And he did. His parents bore his body out of the camp on a travois and, true to Sioux custom, mounted his body on a scaffold facing the sky.[18] Legend has it that an eagle came to rest on Crazy Horse's coffin.[19]

## LARGER THAN LIFE

Larry McMurtry opens his brief biography of Crazy Horse with a passage about the super-sized sculpture of him that is being created. McMurtry notes its impressive size and the lifelong labor of the sculptors. He also comments that it may be one of the only places, if not the only place, where Indians who visit come away smiling.[20] For a broken people whose dreams have been shattered countless times, first by military force, later by government intervention, and finally by the ravages of self-destructive behaviors induced by life on the reservation, Crazy Horse stands above it all, both physically and metaphorically. Never a chief but always a warrior, Crazy Horse was a good provider and protector to his people when he lived and is an inspiration to his people in myth as in life.

# Lessons in Leadership Motivation

- *Know your mission.* Crazy Horse lived (and died) by the vision he had experienced as a young man, in which it was predicted that he would fight for his people and eventually be hurt by them.
- *Put the needs of the tribe first.* Crazy Horse kept little or nothing for himself. He shared the fruits of his hunts and the bounty of his raids with his tribe.
- *Establish your credentials as a leader.* Crazy Horse was an expert hunter as well as a fierce warrior.
- *Be humble.* Crazy Horse deflected glory from himself. He wore only a single feather and little war paint.
- *Sacrifice for the greater good.* Crazy Horse was at home on the prairie and wanted to live out his days there, but when his people were suffering, he headed into the agency to save them, even though he knew that it would be the end of the way of life he loved.

C H A P T E R

"My job is to get my men through all right. Super-
human effort isn't worth a damn unless it achieves
results."

*Ernest Shackleton*
*Explorer*

# INSPIRE

## BEACONS OF INSPIRATION

*I*MAGINE! *He was born into a home in modest circumstances.*
*His father was an alcoholic and had trouble holding a job,*
*so money was always tight. As a young man, he served as*
*a lifeguard, and while doing so saved 77 swimmers from drown-*
*ing. He applied his earnings to pay his way through college.*
*His first job was in radio, but an itch to go west led him to*

*Hollywood, where he became a contract player for a movie studio and made more than 50 pictures, receiving some good reviews as an actor. An interest in politics led him to become active in union politics, and he rose to become president of that union. This activism did not help his movie career, so he was forced to take a job in television, not a step up in those days, when the entertainment industry revolved around moviemaking. Still, he made the best of it and honed his skills as a speaker, making corporate speeches. Ideas that he honed in his stump speeches took him into state politics. And it is in the political arena, where his opponents underestimated him, that he made his greatest impact on the nation and the world. He was Ronald Reagan, fortieth president of the United States. If his life had been a movie script, it never would have sold. But as a genuine life, it was one of remarkable achievement against incredible odds. Why? Consider his attributes.*

- Optimism. *Reagan always looked on the bright side of life. He saw opportunity where others saw despair. He believed in the American dream because he had lived it, personally and on the screen. He was able to take that message to public life, where he found a populace burdened by defeats abroad, soaring inflation at home, and loss of confidence in government.*

- Resilience. *Reagan had an ability to overcome adversity. He grew up with an alcoholic father, but he did not let that hold him back. He earned a scholarship, then a radio contract, and finally a movie contract. He was elected president of the Screen Actors Guild, and he used that position as a platform to protect his industry against both perceived communist influence and over-reaction to that perception. His movie career stalled, but he found a home on television as a spokesman for General Electric. He toured the country on behalf of the company and met and mingled with everyone, from the shop floor to the top floor. In his political life, he met with success as governor, but he was not nominated for the presidency in 1976. Nonetheless, he persevered, promoting with his message through twice-weekly radio broadcasts, and won election in 1980. Throughout all the tough times of his presidency, he did not let political setbacks deter him. He pushed through. Physically he persevered, too. He survived an assassination attempt as well as a bout with cancer and a fall from a horse.*

- Resolve. *He held to his ideas—what Margaret Thatcher called his "big" ideas.[1] He did not bend; he pushed those ideas hard. At times obstinate, he clung to his belief in lower taxes, smaller government, strong defense, and anticommunism. On three counts he was successful; however, the federal government was larger when he left office than when he entered.*

- Perseverance. *Resiliency and resolve emerged from his willingness to persevere. He had a dream of becoming a Hollywood actor, and he became one. He had a dream of entering political life, and he achieved it. He had a dream of setting forth a new conservative agenda, and he implemented it. He also persevered in his battles with ill health and injury, including an assassination attempt that nearly killed him.*

- Charm. *Reagan oozed charm. In part it was due to his charisma; he was a handsome man with a firm bearing and a big smile. But underlying his charisma was a sense of charm that brought people to him. Jack Kennedy was charismatic and likable, but not affable. Reagan had an ability to connect with people on a very personal level and make them feel important; it is a politician's gift. But with Reagan it seemed to come from his "aw shucks, I'm one of you" attitude.*

- Humor. *A key to Reagan's charm was, of course, his humor. Surprisingly, much of the coverage on the week-*

*end of his death noted his humor. Many people focused on the one-liners he dropped, but also mentioned the humor he displayed with them in their individual dealings with him. While many of the stories he told he knew by heart and had used many times, he had the ability to drop a funny story when asked and also to engage people with his own humor. Congressman Christopher Cox, once Reagan's legal counsel, said that the president used to visit the staff in the back of Air Force One to tell stories, as if, said Cox, he believed that it was his job to buck up the people who worked for him.[2]*

- Hope. *Above all, Reagan radiated hope. It was the mainspring of his life, and in 1980 he shared that hope with a nation that had been battered by the Vietnam war and the Iranian hostage affair, as well as economic malaise. He pointed out America's virtues and made people feel good about those virtues and about themselves. The early years of his presidency were not that successful; the economy did not begin to rebound until 1982, and its effect was not immediately apparent. He also radiated that sense of hope to other nations, in particular to Eastern Europe.*

All of these attributes were held together by Reagan's ability to communicate. He worked hard on his written and oral communications. He was a persuasive and often eloquent writer, and he worked long and hard on his speeches. He honed his acting technique and applied it to the podium. Reagan had the ready quip, and while much of what he said was scripted, he could banter with people and make small talk. He was genuinely affable. His greatest failing may have been a disconnect between his affability and his executive ability. He delegated a great deal, and some of the people to whom he delegated took advantage of him or used his ideas to further their own agenda.

History will laud Reagan for his ability to mobilize people around his agenda and ideas, but it will take him to task for his failings. Still, as was apparent after his death, his stature has *risen over time. In part this is because some of his ideas were sound; for example, his emphasis on a strong defense helped to end the Cold War, and his commitment to lower taxes stimulated economic growth. Current and future leaders will be wise to take Reagan's virtues of optimism, resilience, resolve, perseverance, humor, and hope to heart and apply them. Taken together, these attributes enable leaders to inspire their people and lead them, as Reagan tried to do throughout his public life, to the "shining city on the hill." Imagine, indeed!*

🖙 🖙

*The turning of a page in history can sometimes come down to a single moment when the voices of reason come to be heard above the voices of hatred. Such is the case with Rosa Parks. Although shy and soft-spoken by nature, she refused to surrender her seat on a Montgomery, Alabama, bus, and her refusal electrified the civil rights movement. Her moment of defiance was not an impulse; it was a deeply felt act by a righteous woman who understood that that defiance meant arrest. For a black woman in Alabama in the 1950s, going to jail was an act of monumental courage. When Parks called her mother from jail, the first thing her distraught mother asked was, "Did they beat you?"*[3]

*Rosa Parks demonstrated her courage, as well as her sense of adventure, from an early age. She recalls in her autobiography,* Rosa Parks: My Story, *sitting at her grandfather's knee while he waited, shotgun in hand, in case any Klansmen came calling. "I remember thinking that whatever happened, I wanted to see it. I wanted to see him shoot that gun." She was six years old.*[4] *With that attitude, it was no wonder that she found herself attracted to the NAACP; as a young married woman in Montgomery, she became secretary to the local chapter.*

*Her refusal to move from the whites-only section sparked the Montgomery bus boycott, which lasted nearly a year. During that time, blacks refused to ride the buses; instead, they formed ad hoc ride-share committees and, more importantly, forged a spirit of unity that would soon galvanize the civil rights movement as it moved across the South. A young preacher who had recently moved to the city rose to prominence during the boycott. His name was Martin Luther King, Jr. While King would transcend Montgomery, taking the cause of civil rights to the nation, Mrs. Parks saw no immediate benefit. She and her husband, Raymond, who was also active in civil rights, were forced to leave the city; they headed for Detroit.[5]*

*Douglas Brinkley, her biographer, writes that Mrs. Parks was "the spiritual essence of the civil rights movement. . . . This demure, dainty woman exposed the true ugliness of the Jim Crow South."[6] Morris Dees, founder of the Southern Poverty Law Center, says, "When the history of the civil rights movement is written 100 years from now, there are only going to be two significant names, Martin Luther King and Rosa Parks."[7]*

*Rosa Parks's commitment to civil rights did not end in Montgomery. After moving to Detroit, she remained active in civil rights activities, helping a young black civil rights activist campaign for Congress. John Conyers won and immediately hired Mrs. Parks, who served as one of his administrative assistants for 23 years until her retirement in 1988, at the age of 75.*

*Retirement did not slow Mrs. Parks; she founded a "mentoring organization for teenagers" and remained a visible and vibrant presence in the civil rights community well into her eighties and nineties.[8] Her legacy also continues in another way: The Rosa Parks Scholarship Fund awards $2,000 grants annually to students who, in addition to good academic performance and "need," demonstrate a commitment to "community service." More than a million dollars in scholarships has been awarded to over 500 students since the fund was established in 1980, a fitting tribute to a worthy woman of conscience.[9]*

⋙ ⋘

Inspire. Its original meaning was to "breathe or blow upon or into." The word was derived from the Latin *spiritus*, which means "breath, courage, vigor, the soul" as well as from the Ecclesiastical Latin *spirare*, meaning "to blow, breathe."[10] How apt! When you think of how leaders inspire, it is as if they are "blowing life into" their people to give courage and vigor to their souls. Ronald Reagan blew life into the American people, instilling a renewed sense of confidence and possibility. Rosa Parks blew life into the civil rights movement by refusing to give up her seat to a white man. The "life" that each gave was a form of hope. Hope is the outcome of inspiration.

Hope is not something you wish for; it must be earned through example and courage. It emerges from a unity of spirit and purpose. Sun Tzu, the ancient military strategist, addressed the need for a commander and his army to be one with the *Tao*. As he explained in the *Art of War*, "Tao is what causes the people to have the same purpose as their superior. Thus they can die with him, live with him and not deceive him."[11] The reason for such unity was a shared purpose that emerged from a shared set of values. It was the commander's responsibility to earn the respect of his soldiers so that they would follow him into battle if war were necessary.

One of the reasons we heed Sun Tzu's words today is that so much of what he wrote, or dictated to others, was about avoiding conflict and resorting to battle only as a last resort. Sun Tzu then inspired his people by example. His military strategies remain valid today, but his lessons on the Tao as a unity of purpose are even more timely. Sun Tzu knew how to create conditions that would lead his soldiers to want to follow him. He was a stickler for discipline, but he also put the care and safety of his troops first. It was his example that caused others to follow him, and this is why we read him today, two and a half millennia later. Ernest Shackleton took Sun Tzu's maxims to heart. His example of selflessness, reinforced by what today we would call "random acts of kindness," endeared him to his men and made them willing to do whatever he asked. Why? Because they knew he cared.

## A REASON TO BELIEVE

Another reason that Sun Tzu's words have relevance today is that no matter how grand his strategies or how sound his tactics, he understood, as all good leaders today do, that nothing is possible without the support of others. And while Sun Tzu's troops needed to have attention paid to their physical needs, they also, like employees today, needed to have attention given to their psychic needs. Employees need and want to believe in their leaders. And it is up to those leaders to give them a reason to believe. Talk to anyone who was ever involved in a successful start-up venture and you will see his eyes light up as he recalls the excitement of developing a new product or service and bringing it to market. Excitement is not reserved for entrepreneurs. Managers in large companies can take equal pride in a new product development, process improvement, or customer service enhancement. Likewise, those who are involved in social services can take pride in helping others get back to health or back into the mainstream of society. All work should have a purpose. Here are some things you can do to create inspiration in the workplace.

- *Set bold goals.* Challenges are motivators. It is up to the leader to inspire others to follow by setting forth a goal that everyone can aspire to achieve. People look to their leaders for inspiration in good times and in bad. Inspiration is built upon self-motivation, but it is nurtured by the example of the leader and others in the organization who are trying to excel.

- *Develop narrative business plans.* The act of transforming facts and figures into stories makes them more understandable. When people can experience through a story what might happen if they follow the business plan, they have a tendency to become excited about what they can do and will do. Rubbermaid and 3M have made a practice of this. Royal Dutch Shell pioneered the concept of scenario planning, or putting forecasts into narratives. While it is well known that Shell had produced a scenario depicting the OPEC oil cartel, it is less well known that the company continues the practice today because it finds it valuable. (*Hint:* Put data into the appendix. People need access to them as a means of measuring progress—that is, do the numbers prove that we are doing what we said we would do?)

- *Tell stories of great people.* Just as narrative business plans work as motivators, so, too, do stories. Since time immemorial we have listened to stories of our elders. Indigenous peoples everywhere use stories of their ancients to provide explanations of the present and serve as a means of giving guidance for the future. Today we still enjoy stories. The most popular management and motivational speakers use stories to convey their points. Why? Because stories are a way to give direction and insight without platitudes and prescriptions. Hearing how Thomas Watson built the sales force at IBM, how Sam Walton created Wal-Mart from a small five-and-dime, or how Michael Dell created a computer empire from his college dormitory is exciting. We find ourselves inspired by such stories. Many high-performing organizations tell stories of their people, as we pointed out in the previous chapter. Stories of people who are like us and who achieve serve to motivate us to follow their example.

- *Create discovery sessions.* One of the best ways for people to find inspiration is to get outside of themselves. Travel is a wonderful way to experience different cultures; leaders of global businesses often return to their home offices with new ideas about how to handle problems. A way to create the sensation of travel without leaving the city is to arrange for an off-site meeting for a team or department. The session will focus on creativity or innovation and will be an opportunity for people to experience new things in order to stimulate their own creative thinking. Exercises can include vision maps, where people talk about where they want their organization to go and translate those ideas into images. Root Learning of Maumee, Ohio, is one of the leading developers of such pictograms. Root has worked with a who's who of global companies, and the methods that Root uses are designed to harness the creativity of the team and make it accessible to everyone in the organization.

• *Think outside your field.* Another way to stimulate creativity and contribute to inspiration is to encourage people to look at other businesses. The automotive industry adopted this tactic as a means of educating and training dealers in the benefits of good customer service. For many of us, buying a car and having it serviced is a singularly unpleasant experience. To help orient their dealers toward a positive customer service experience, the auto companies profiled the guest experiences pioneered by noted customer-friendly companies like the Walt Disney Company and Ritz-Carlton. Trainers from these companies even came and spoke to dealer groups. As a result, dealers began to understand customer expectations and to strive to deliver a better customer experience. Another industry that has undergone a similar transformation is health care. Hospitals have invested millions in providing a customer-friendly experience for patients and their families. The practice of looking outside of oneself is inherent in science. Research scientists specialize in a particular subject, but some great breakthroughs have come when a researcher looked at phenomena in another area and applied the lessons learned there to her own specialty. Such cross-pollination facilitates development of new drugs, new treatments, and ultimately cures for disease.

* *Encourage optimism.* Inspiration comes to those who have an open spirit. "Optimism is an essential ingredient for innovation," wrote Robert Noyce, cofounder of Intel.

"How else can the individual welcome change over security, adventure over staying in his safe places?" Noyce, a gifted engineer and research scientist, was also a keen leader of others. "People come here [to Intel] because of their abilities. My job [is] to remove all impediments to progress and give them as much freedom as possible."[12]

## FINDING INSPIRATION

Inspiration lies at the root of motivation. After all, it is what gives us the gumption to get going, especially during times of change, of stress, or just plain doldrums. To be able to think of things and people. Inspiration can come from anywhere at any time.

Like brainstorming, inspiration can be encouraged. You can consciously put yourself into situations where thoughts of greatness surround you. For example, walk the grounds of a famous battlefield. Gettysburg is a popular destination for students of leadership. Stand where General Robert E. Lee stood as he surveyed the battlefield. Stroll to the top of Little Round Top, where Colonel Joshua Chamberlain turned the tide of battle for the Union. And walk the ground where Major General George E. Pickett made his fateful charge, effectively ending the South's last hope of victory.

A trip to an art museum will let you peek into the minds of creative geniuses who expressed their vision on canvas or in stone. Likewise, a visit to a museum of technology will fill you with the wonder of innovation. Or if nature is your thing, hike into the mountains or walk along the seacoast. Drink in the majesty of the natural splendor that man did not create, but can help to preserve. A stroll in a forest may have the same effect. Horizons are limited, but the imagination is not. Everywhere you look there is life of every sort struggling to make its mark. The point is that inspiration is all around us. It is our responsibility as leaders to rejuvenate ourselves with ideas from everywhere. For some, those ideas will come from books. For others, they will come from observing people. For all of us, the ideas must be put to use so that we keep up our spirits in order to give something of ourselves to the next generation.

## INSPIRED LEADERSHIP

When it comes to leadership, however, the genuine and lasting inspiration comes from those who lead others, rallying them to a cause greater than they might otherwise have dreamed of. Recall the words of Henry V on the eve of battle with the French, where the English were outnumbered four to one:

> We few, we happy few, we band of brothers;
> For he today that sheds his blood with me
> Shall be my brother, be he ne'er so vile,
> This day shall gentle his condition:
> And gentlemen in England and now a-bed
> Shall think themselves accursed they were not here,
> And hold their manhoods cheap, while any speaks
> That fought with us.[13]

As this passage from Shakespeare illustrates, inspiration emerges from raised expectations. And when expectations are raised and nurtured by genuine leadership, great results can and will occur.

## GIVING HOPE

What inspiration really comes down to is this: giving hope. Motivation thrives on hope; it is the spirit that makes belief in tomorrow possible. With hope, individuals can see over the edge of adversity; they can look beyond where they stand now. All of the leaders profiled in this book are men and women who give or gave hope throughout their lives. They were able to impart hope by setting the right example, communicating effectively, empowering their followers, coaching regularly, recognizing frequently, and making sacrifices for the organization. The hope they shared with their people fueled the spirit of motivation. But while leaders impart hope, ultimately it is the followers who must adopt hope and make it their own. Without hope, nothing is possible. With hope, everything is possible.

---

## Insights into Motivation: Mary Parker Follett

Mary Parker Follett, who was trained as a social worker, was a management theorist before her time. Writing in the twenties and thirties, she viewed management as a balance of people and operations. She was most interested in the people side of the equation. In *Dynamic Administration*, a collection of essays published in 1941, Follett wrote, "Responsibility is the greatest developer of men." According to management author Stuart Cranier, Follett viewed a "leader as someone who sees the whole rather than the particular." She wrote that "We should never allow ourselves to be bullied by 'either-or.' There is often the possibility of something better than either of two given alternatives." Follett's form of holistic leadership focused on people as contributors who can and should be encouraged to develop their talents and capabilities.[14]

---

## Motivation Planner: Inspire

To inspire others is to lead them to a better place. It is essential to motivation. Use the following questions to see how you might foster inspiration in your work environment.

(*Continued on next page.*)

1. Consider the goals of your organization. Are they bold? If so, why? What would happen if you made them grander?

2. Think about your business objectives for the coming year. How could you tell a story about what you want to accomplish? Be certain to include how you will know when you have achieved your objectives.

3. Think about the people who have inspired you. How can you share stories about them with your people? Invite others to share stories of people who have inspired them.

4. What kinds of things can you do with your people to stimulate their creativity?
   - Arrange for a field trip to a museum.
   - Hire a guest speaker.
   - Do a volunteer project for a school or social service agency.

5. What lessons can you learn from other businesses or professions? Can you invite people from those businesses and professions to speak to your people? Are there books about them that you might read that would be of value to your people?

6. What things can you do in your organization to help people look on the bright side? What reasons can you give them to be optimistic?

7. Where will you find your own sources of inspiration?

8. What can you do to give hope to the people with whom you work?

## SIR ERNEST SHACKLETON

One of the most remarkable photographs ever taken during an expedition does not seem at all remarkable upon first viewing.

But when you learn the story behind the photograph, you get a glimpse into the heart of a man who has gone down in history as one of the most remarkable motivators of all time. The photograph is of men playing soccer on the pack ice; in the background is their ship, frozen at a dead stop.[15] It is the HMS *Endurance,* which was under the direction of Sir Ernest Shackleton, the expedition leader. At the time this photograph was taken, the crew's situation was bad, but over the coming year it would grow progressively worse. Why they were playing a game at a time of danger lies at the heart of Shackleton's ability to lead. It comes down to a single word: morale.

Ernest Shackleton was a man of his times, but in many ways he was also a leader who was well ahead of his era. He came of age in the time of Victoria, and while he was an Irishman, he was steeped in the legacy of Empire. He yearned to explore; as a young man, he made treks to both the Arctic and the Antarctic, and was in fact with Sir Robert Scott's expedition to find the South Pole. That expedition ended fatally for Scott, but it only stirred Shackleton to try to be the first to traverse the barren continent. Unlike Scott, a fiercely proud but autocratic leader, Shackleton was what we would today call an empowering leader; he delegated to his subordinates, much preferring a style of self-directed teams. He was not even the captain of the *Endurance*; Frank A. Worsley was. But make no mistake, Shackleton was in full command of the expedition, as the name by which he was known implies— "Boss."

## THE VOYAGE SOUTHWARD

The first step in the journey south was to raise funds and assemble an expeditionary team. In his book about this adventure, *South: The Endurance Expedition*, Shackleton includes portions of the prospectus he used to, as he says, "arouse the interest of the general public." The document clearly states the exploratory (first to cross the Antarctic) and scientific (biological and geological) natures of the expedition.[16] What the document does not contain is Shackleton's zeal for exploration; he reserved that for his public lectures and private fundraising sessions.[17] As he confided to F. A. Worsley, the captain of the *Endurance*, much later about his polar expeditions, "If you are once in it, heart and soul, as you are and I am, you can never devote yourself thoroughly to anything else. At the back of your mind there is always the ice—the ice and the hope of finding what lies beyond it."[18]

After raising the necessary funds, the expedition set off from Plymouth, England, in August 1914—not a fortunate time to be leaving for the South Pole. War was imminent, and, to his credit, Shackleton volunteered the services of his ship and his crew to the Admiralty, asking only that they be allowed serve as a unit. He was given permission to proceed; no one could have foreseen the terrible carnage that was to ensue in the coming months and years. Later, Shackleton received much criticism for leaving Britain on the eve of war, and it dogged him for the rest of his life. Upon his return to civilization, Shackleton did enlist in the war effort, as did some of his crew, three of whom lost their lives in the conflict.[19]

## GOING WITH THE (ICE) FLOES

It had been Shackleton's plan to winter either in a harbor on the Weddell Sea or on South Georgia Island, but the ice was unusually heavy in late 1914 and early 1915 (summer months in the Antarctic), and the *Endurance* became trapped in the ice pack. What follows from there is an adventure as exciting as anything ever dreamt of by a Hollywood screenwriter. Even today, with the distance of time, it was an adventure of unprecedented magnitude. The ship was 400 miles from Antarctica, 500 miles from a Swedish supply station, and 1,000 miles from South Georgia Island. A steamer like the *Endurance* could conceivably survive being stuck; what she could not survive was the shifting of the ice pack that would occur with the spring thaw. And she did not; she was crushed and sank, but not before Shackleton had made the decision to abandon ship and bring as many of the provisions as possible.[20]

It is here that Shackleton reveals his flexibility. In his own account of abandoning *Endurance*, Shackleton betrays no hint of his dismay at missing his big opportunity to traverse Antarctica. Worsley, however, records the pain of the moment for Shackleton, but notes Shackleton's immediate shift of priorities: "It is a pity [to miss the crossing], but that cannot be helped. It is the men we have to think about." This was the moment when Shackleton shifted all the energy that had been focused on exploration into energy that was focused on survival, and in so doing he proved that he was masterful in his understanding of what needed to be done on both a strategic and a personal level. So what did Shackleton do? He ordered the raising of the Union Jack as a means of bucking up his men's spirits and uniting them as well as linking them to the Empire, which was engaged in war. While they were not fighting an enemy, they were fighting to survive. A short time later, he ordered each man to keep only two pounds of personal possessions. Since they would have to trek across the ice pack dragging boats and supplies, weight was at a premium. But instead of arbitrarily making decisions for his men, he let them decide; after all, the men would need something personal to cling to in the harrowing months ahead. Worsley notes that Shackleton did encourage one crewman to keep his banjo, and it was lucky for him that he did, because that crewman was able to keep the rest of the crew entertained.[21]

Entertainment is a refrain that appears in all the narratives of the expedition. Prior to the *Endurance*'s sinking, the men created a room that they called the Ritz, where they held parties and shows. On the ice, the men kept themselves occupied by reading books that they had retrieved from the ship, even referring to the *Encyclopedia Britannica* to settle lively arguments over scientific or historical facts. Humor, too, played a role, with Shackleton telling stories or teasing his men. What Shackleton was doing was keeping his men alive inside; by encouraging them to read or sing, he was keeping their spirits from sagging or dwelling on the inhospitalities that in other circumstances might have overwhelmed them.[22]

## ELEPHANT ISLAND

After five months on the ice, the men reached Elephant Island. For the first time in a year they were on land—as barren and inhospitable as it was, it was, nonetheless, land. But almost immediately Shackleton realized that they did not have enough provisions to survive, so he would have to do something that he had heretofore resisted: split the group. He would lead a rescue team to South Georgia Island, where he could enlist the help of a whaling ship to bring the remaining crew members home. A testament to Shackleton's leadership was revealed later by Frank Wild, who stayed behind as team leader on Elephant Island. He emulated the Boss's example by invoking his name and his methods as a means of keeping those who stayed behind focused on survival.[23]

## ACROSS TO SOUTH GEORGIA

The distance from Elephant Island to South Georgia Island is 800 miles; the journey is across rolling oceans with howling winds. Six men made the journey in a small boat, the *James Cairn*, alternating two-hour shifts of navigating, manning the pump, and resting. This part of the story illuminates Shackleton at his finest. He insisted on regular hot meals and regularly served hot beverages. One reason was fitness; he needed his men well nourished. The second reason was emotional; he sought always to buoy the spirits of his men, to keep them upbeat throughout the perilous journey. In fact, in Shackleton's own account of the expedition, the topic of food is woven throughout the narrative. Shackleton used food as a motivator. Worsley notes that Shackleton doled out treats in the form of sugar or nougat. It was a way of injecting a kind of normalcy into the abnormal, but it is also deeply indicative of Shackleton's selflessness. There is an account of his actions when the team was on the ice floe and part of the crew had gone back to retrieve supplies. What did Shackleton do? A mile from the camp, he and another crewman greeted the returnees with hot tea. This was not an isolated example; such niceties occur throughout the narratives.[24]

The *James Cairn* eventually reached South Georgia, but Shackleton and his men discovered that they were on the opposite side of the island from the whaling station. Shackleton did not despair; choosing Worsley and another crewman, he trekked across the island, thought then to be "inaccessible." The journey, up the side of a mountain and across ice and yawning crevices, often in the dark, took 36 hours. When Shackleton stumbled into Husvik, the whaling station, he encountered two children, who took one look at the three bearded men in torn and soiled clothes who had not bathed in 18 months, and ran. Fortunately, Shackleton found the station master, who greeted him warmly. Their homecoming was not without sadness; Shackleton recalled learning for the first time that the war was still raging and had taken the lives of millions.[25]

## THE RESCUE

As exhausted as Shackleton was by the arduous journey that he had just experienced, he insisted on going back to retrieve his men on Elephant Island. As with everything in this adventure, nothing went as planned. It took him four tries to get from South Georgia Island to Elephant Island; bad weather had hindered the rescue. But as he neared the coast, he called out, "Are you all well?" To which came the reply that he had hoped to hear for the past year and a half: "We are all well, Boss." Shackleton had done it; he had brought all of his men home safely. Considering the magnitude of the challenge of being trapped in the ice, living on a barren island, crossing 800 miles of open ocean, and then trekking across a glacier to safety, it is remarkable that he succeeded. That he did it is an extraordinary testament to a man who understood not only what needed to be done, but how it was to be done: by keeping his crew motivated in spite of the overwhelming odds.[26]

## A LEADER OF MEN

In his closing chapter on the journey, Worsley, who clearly idealized Shackleton, summed up his feelings this way:

And what of him as a man? I recalled the way in which he had led his party across the ice-floes after the *Endurance* had been lost; how, by his genius for leadership he had kept us all in health; how, by the sheer force of his personality he had kept our spirits up; and how by his magnificent example, he had enabled us to win through when the die of the elements were loaded against us.[27]

Later in the same chapter, Worsley quotes a crewman as writing, "[Shackleton] had a way of compelling loyalty. . . .We would have gone anywhere without question just on his order."[28] One way in which Shackleton encouraged loyalty was by keeping his men united in purpose. For example, he would shift men from tent to tent to keep dissension from building. As a result, as Worsley notes, "Of loyalty toward his leadership there was never any question."[29] The reason Shackleton's men felt so strongly about him was that he led from his heart and his spirit; he was firm in his purpose, but he was always kind and always resourceful in finding ways to alleviate the hardships in the pursuit of their goals.

While Shackleton died at the close of an age when explorers made front-page news, his leadership lessons remain as contemporary as today's all-news cable updates. The reason is that he did what all great leaders do: He put the needs of his crew ahead of his own. In big things (such as sailing in a small boat across an open sea) and little things (like celebrating Christmas), Shackleton earned the hearts and minds of his men. And by winning their confidence and trust, he was able to save each and every one of them. He was truly a leader of remarkable character!

---

## Lessons in Leadership Motivation

- *Bend the vision.* When Shackleton knew that crossing the Antarctic was out of reach, he immediately shifted to the plan of saving his men.

- *Do the heavy sledding.* Shackleton shared the physical labors as well as the watches.

- *Share the biscuits.* Shackleton would forgo his own rations in order to feed the undernourished or the ill. And he often did so without anyone knowing it.

- *Know your men.* Shackleton allowed his crew to choose what valuables were most important to them.

- *Look for opportunities to buck people up.* Shackleton doled out nougat and sugar as treats to keep his men energized as well as motivated.

- *Put people first.* Shackleton always put the needs of his men ahead of his personal comfort, and as a result he saved them all.

# FINAL THOUGHT: A RESPONSIBILITY TO MOTIVATE

*T*HE PHRASE *"FAILURE OF LEADERSHIP"* echoed through the Senate chamber that day in the spring of 2004 as Major General Antonio Taguba described the conditions in Abu Ghraib prison that had led to the abuses of Iraqi prisoners. Leaving aside the culpability of the soldiers who had perpetrated the crimes, it was curious to note that the accused soldiers all said that they were doing what was asked of them. Soldiers up and down the chain of command spoke of a pressure to get intelligence from the prisoners, and as a result the civil rights of people in custody were trampled. Some of the prisoners may have been terrorists, but many more were not. What is certain, however, is that the actions that resulted were caused by a failure of command. The higher-ups had failed to create conditions in *which prison guards observed accepted protocols in dealing with prisoners. Either deliberately or through negligence, the higher-ups had failed to create conditions in which human dignity was preserved. As a result, both prisoners and guards suffered: the prisoners suffered the abuse, and the guards suffered the punishment of the law. Both groups were treated poorly by civilian and military commanders who either chose to look the other way or fostered criminal abuse.*

*Back in the United States, we have seen a failure of leadership in corporate governance. Senior leaders of organizations have put their desire for wealth ahead of the rights of shareholders, vendors, and employees. Sometimes the CEOs were outright crooks, looting as much as they could. Other times, boards made up of the CEO's cronies failed to look beyond the balance sheet to judge the effect of fiscal mismanagement. Employees, too, were sucked into the improprieties; some were convicted and sent to prison, well in advance of the higher-ups, who could afford better legal advice. In the end, the entire corporation suffered. Customers went unserved, shareholders suffered investment losses, and vendors went unpaid; worst of all, innocent employees were laid off or incurred losses in wages and retirement benefits.*

*In Iraq and in the United States, senior managers created conditions in which abuse of privilege occurred, and as a result the only motivation was the urge to flee. Indeed, these are examples of a failure in leadership.*

☙ ❧

The focus of this book has been on the positive—specifically, on what leaders can do to create conditions in which people will motivate themselves: set the right example, communicate clearly, challenge judiciously, empower appropriately, coach frequently, recognize with meaning, and sacrifice for the total good. Not everyone can do all of these things, but the more of them that you do, the better the results. The net result is an inspired workplace:

People feel good about their leadership and about themselves. They want to do a good job.

## LEADERSHIP RESPONSIBILITY

The opposite is also true. When management turns a blind eye to the needs of its employees for whatever reason, be it deliberate or inadvertent, it sends a message to its people. The message is, "We Don't Care." That message is as clear as a corporate logo and as loud as any commercial jingle. It is a message that resonates in the hallways, the break rooms, and the cafeterias. About the only place it does not seem to resonate is in the boardroom; too often, the senior leaders of companies with demotivated workforces do not seem to care about what their people need or want. Of if they do care, they assume that they cannot afford to give them those things. Actually, the opposite is true. Aside from compensation and benefits, which are costly, much of what binds people to their place of work is not costly. It does not cost more to set the right example, communicate frequently, delegate authority, coach with conviction, or recognize achievements. But to avoid doing those things can be costly, because what you lose is commitment. A committed worker will take the extra step to do things correctly, whether it is working longer hours to meet a deadline, making phone calls to customers, or being willing to embrace change in order to do things better, faster, more efficiently, and for less cost. Those things cannot be purchased with a paycheck; they can be paid for only by the commitment of management to employee.

## EMPLOYEE RESPONSIBILITY

Employees have a responsibility, too. While management creates the conditions in which motivation can occur, employees must respond to those conditions. They need to open themselves up to the examples of communication, coaching, challenging, and recognition. If examples of the leaders living the values or sacrificing for the organization fail to inspire, then the fault may lie with the employee. He may not be connecting because he does not want to work in that business. However, when management is genuinely leading, employees owe the organization their best effort. If an employee cannot give that effort, then she is not fulfilling her end of the bargain. She should look for other opportunities in another department or another line of work. For example, if an employee is working in the accounting department of a manufacturing company, but he would rather be doing social work for a school district, then no amount of conditioning, no amount of motivation, no amount of leadership will make him happy. Only a career change will improve the dynamic.

Motivation, as mentioned earlier, is a two-way street. The leaders profiled in this book demonstrated by example how to create conditions in which motivation can flourish, but equally, the men and women who served with these leaders responded to their leadership and motivated themselves to respond to the challenges. As a result, the leaders pushed and pulled their organizations forward, to the benefit of their people. Some, like Crazy Horse and Ernest Shackleton, did not enjoy the fruits of their labors, but others, like Mary Kay Ash, Colleen Barrett, David Hackworth, Sam Walton, Pat Summitt, Thich Nhat Hanh, and the rest, did enjoy them. For all of these leaders, their ability to influence the lives of others positively will be their lasting legacy.

# SECRETS OF CREATING AN INSPIRED WORKPLACE FOR OTHERS AND YOURSELF

## RAISING AND FULFILLING EXPECTATIONS FOR YOUR PEOPLE

*Creating the conditions in which motivation can occur may be one of the most formidable challenges you will face as a manager. The theory and practice provided in this book, buttressed by the examples of real-life motivators, can provide you with ideas that you can put to good use. A way to create ideal motivational conditions is to raise expectations for yourself, your team, and your organization, and then devote yourself to finding ways for everyone to fulfill those expectations. In doing so you want to make the expectations as specific and concrete as possible so that your people know what they are striving to attain The following suggestions will help you get started.*[1]

## Exemplify Integrity

- Do what you say you will do.

- Insist that everyone live the values of the company.

- Live your own values.

## Communicate Relentlessly

- Speak as a leader. Remember, your words represent the views of the entire organization.

- Listen as a leader. Check for understanding and solicit feedback.

- Learn as a leader. Consider what you see, hear, and observe. Incorporate the good ideas of others into your own actions.

## Challenge with Creativity

- Identify challenges that will increase the talents and skills of your people.

- Look for ways to develop cross-functional responsibilities.

- Foster the creative talents of your people by exposing them to new and different experiences that are designed to excite their imagination.

- Enable your people to meet and mingle with people from other departments.[2]

*Empower with Vigor*

- Delegate responsibility.
- Confer authority.
- Hold yourself and the people who work for you accountable for their words, actions, and deeds.
- Make yourself invisible in good times and visible in tough times.

*Coach Frequently*

- Listen first, praise next, critique last.
- Gain agreement for improvement.
- Follow through and follow up on all agreements.
- Teach others to coach.

*Recognize Meaningfully*

- Praise people in front of their peers.
- Reward people with recognition that matters.
- Share stories of heroes of the organization.
- Affirm the dignity of individuals and the work they do.

*Sacrifice with Honor*

- Put the needs of the team first.
- Share the pain.
- Make the sacrifice count for something.

*Inspire by Example*

- Be the first to volunteer for tough assignments.
- Lead from the front.
- When times get tough, be seen and heard frequently.

# RAISING AND FULFILLING YOUR OWN EXPECTATIONS

## TIPS ON MOTIVATING YOURSELF

Every day people get up in the morning and do incredible things. Athletes rise and put themselves through rigorous exercises for hours on end. Salespeople greet the day by calling on their customers, and often close it the same way. Teachers come to class each day to educate our children. Police officers and firefighters put themselves on the line every time they don the uniform. Soldiers meet each day with the recognition that the unexpected may occur at any moment. Managers find that morning may bring a new set of issues, some of which are wholly unforeseen. But with each of these situations comes the realization that challenges bring opportunity, if you have the right mindset. That mindset is one that is rooted in the concept of personal leadership, which you can consider to be the willingness to make a positive difference, coupled with a sense of autonomy, initiative, and responsibility.[3] A driving factor in personal leadership is self-motivation.

The focus of this book has been on what leaders can to do establish conditions in which people can motivate themselves. Now it is time to turn the tables and focus on what you need to do to motivate yourself. The lessons of the leaders profiled in this book can point you in the right direction. Their guidance on how they motivate their people can be turned inward to raise and fulfill your own expectations. Use their lessons to motivate yourself. Here are some specifics that you can use to motivate yourself and achieve your own leadership goals.

*Exemplify*

- Set goals. Ask yourself where you want to go, and map a strategy for getting there.

- Keep on schedule. Focus on what needs doing in your life, and do it. Don't put off doing important things that need doing right away.

- Prioritize the tasks for each day. Keep tabs on what you do and what you postpone. Revisit your priorities daily.

- Look at the role models in your life. Consider why you admire and respect them. Determine whether there are any characteristics they have that you could incorporate into your own life.

- Set a good example for others. See what effect your good example has on others. Remember what you see and keep doing it.

*Communicate*

- Create your purpose statement, i.e., why you do what you do. Review it periodically to make certain that it reflects your current aspirations and desires.

- Make a habit of listening to others more actively. Make certain that people understand what you are saying. If they do not, commit to becoming a more active listener by making eye contact, asking questions, and restating what you have heard.

- Learn from what you see and hear. If you come across a good idea that may improve your own life, adopt it. Pay attention to mistakes; remember what you did and how you can avoid making the same mistake the next time.

*Challenge*

- Look for challenges that will develop your talents, i.e., what you are good at doing.

- Look for jobs that will enable you to develop your skills, i.e., seek cross-functional assignments.

- Look for the next challenge. Embrace the fear that it may provoke. A little fear is good for the soul. Channel that fear so that you can use it to your advantage as a motivator to succeed.[4]

- Look for ways to stimulate your creativity. Such ways include reading, going to the movies, and traveling.

## Empower

- Give yourself permission to accept the next leadership challenge that comes your way. Prepare yourself to increase your level of responsibility. Be certain that you have the authority to do what you do.

## Coach

- Make a list of your strengths. Consider why you do these things well and how you could do them even better.

- Make a list of your weaknesses. Pick one and focus on improving it. When you finish that, pick another one. Keep going until you have gone through the entire list. Then repeat the exercise.

## Recognize

- Review your accomplishments of the past six months. Take pride in what you have done.

- Reward yourself by treating yourself to something you like to do—exercise, read, garden, hike, or play a sport. Indulge yourself; you've earned it.

## Sacrifice

- Consider the people in your life who have made sacrifices for you. These may be your parents, your teachers, your coaches, or even a boss. What is it about these sacrifices that means the most to you? Identify what it is and resolve to emulate that example. For instance, if your parents have forgone spending on themselves in order to educate you, consider how you might do the same for your children or for someone else. If a teacher or coach spent extra hours helping you to learn a subject or hone a skill, do the same for someone else.

- Be a mentor to someone. A mentor is a selfless teacher who seeks nothing for himself. The reward is the sharing of something with others.

*Inspire*

- Look at the lives of people who have inspired others to achieve. Consider how they did it and why. What lessons can you draw from their example? Seek to exemplify these virtues in your own life.

# NOTES

## INTRODUCTION

[1] Adapted from multiple sources, including David M. Kennedy, "Victory at Sea, Part 2," *The Atlantic Monthly*, March 1999 (adapted from his book *Freedom from Fear: The American People in Depression and War, 1929–1945* [Oxford University Press, 1999]); Victor Davis Hanson, *Carnage and Culture: Landmark Battles in the Rise of Western Power* (New York: Anchor Books, 2001), pp. 375–388; and "Pilots at the Battle of Midway," available at www.acepilots.com/misc_midway.html.

[2] The author first explored the nature of intrinsic motivation as well as how leaders motivate in a previous work. John Baldoni and Eric Harvey, *180 Ways to Walk the Motivation Talk* (Dallas, Tex.: Walk the Talk Company, 2002).

## CHAPTER 1

[1] Victor Davis Hanson, *Carnage and Culture: Landmark Battles in the Rise of Western Culture* (New York: Anchor Books, 2002 [paperback edition]), pp. 1–5.

[2] Justin Pope, "Malden Mills Emerges from Bankruptcy," Associated Press, Aug. 15, 2003.

[3] Richard Florida, *The Rise of the Creative Class* (New York: Basic Books, 2004), p. 68.

[4] Ibid., pp. 88–96.

[5] Elizabeth G. Chambers, Mark Foulon, Helen Handfield-Jones, Steven M. Hankin, and Edward G. Michaels III, "War for Talent,"

*McKinsey Quarterly* 3 (1998), pp. 44–57, cited in Florida, *Rise of the Creative Class*, pp. 99–100.

[6] Elizabeth L. Axelrod, Helen Handfield-Jones, and Timothy A. Welsh, "War for Talent, Part Two," *McKinsey Quarterly* 2 (2001); abstract available at www.mckinseyquarterly.com.

[7] *The Towers Perrin Talent Report: New Realities in Today's Workplace* (New York: Towers Perrin, 2001), cited in Florida, *Rise of the Creative Class*, p. 100.

[8] Society of Human Resource Management survey of workplace attitudes, October 2003.

[9] Gallup Organization survey, 2003. (Cited in a presentation by Marcus Buckingham at Living Leadership 2003, held Nov. 5, 2003, in Atlanta, Ga.)

[10] Bob Nelson, "The Ironies of Motivation," *Strategy & Leadership*, January/February 1999.

[11] Benedict Carey, "Fear in the Workplace: The Bullying Boss," *New York Times*, June 22, 2004. Among those quoted in the article are Dr. Calvin Morrill of University of California–Irvine; Dr. Harvey A. Hornstein, retired from Columbia University; Dr. Leigh Thompson of Northwestern; and Dr. Bennett Tepper of University of North Carolina–Charlotte. Dr. Michelle Duffy, also quoted, has done research on the effect of the abusive behavior of bosses on others.

[12] Abraham Maslow, *Notes on Management*, foreword by Warren Bennis (New York: John Wiley & Sons, 1998), p. xx.

[13] Kevin Freiberg and Jackie Freiberg, *Nuts! Southwest Airlines Crazy Recipe for Business and Personal Success* (New York: Broadway Books, 1998), p. 27.

[14] Wade Goodwyn, "Profile: Success of Southwest Airlines," *NPR Morning Edition*, Washington, D.C., Dec. 4, 2002.

[15] Katrina Booker, "Herb Kelleher: The Chairman of the Board Looks Back," *Fortune*, May 14, 2001.

[16] Goodwyn, "Profile."

[17] Freiberg and Freiberg, *Nuts!*, p. 201.

[18] Andy Serwer, "Southwest Airlines: The Hottest Thing in the Sky," *Fortune*, Mar. 8, 2004.

[19] Ibid.

[20] Melanie Trottman, "New Atmosphere: Inside Southwest Airlines, Storied Culture Feels Strains," *Wall Street Journal*, July 11, 2003.

[21] Ibid.

[22] Sherri Deatherage Green, "Corporate Case Study: Southwest Airlines Keeps PR Course with Flying Colors," *PR Week*, Jan. 26, 2004.

[23] Freiberg and Freiberg, *Nuts!,* p. 105.

[24] Serwer, "Southwest Airlines."

[25] Green, "Corporate Case Study."

[26] Trottman, "New Atmosphere."

[27] Freiberg and Freiberg, *Nuts!,* p. 310.

[28] Ibid.

[29] Ibid., p. 97.

[30] Ibid.

[31] Clint Swett, "In Tough Times, Southwest Airlines Manages to Fly High," *Knight Ridder Tribune Business News (The Sacramento Bee)*, Washington, D.C., Nov. 24, 2002.

[32] Trottman, "New Atmosphere."

[33] Freiberg and Freiberg, *Nuts!,* pp. 231–232.

[34] Ibid., p. 314.

[35] Ibid., pp. 130–135.

[36] Booker, "Herb Kelleher."

[37] Swett, "Tough Times."

[38] Bill Choyke, "Southwest Flies Its Own Route," *The Virginian-Pilot & The Ledger-Star*, Sept. 15, 2003.

[39] Goodwyn, "Profile."

## CHAPTER 2

[1] José De Cordoba, "Why Susie Krabacher Sold the Sushi Bar to Buy an Orphanage," Mar. 1, 2004.

[2] Joanne Ditmer "Aspen's Angel for Haiti's Ex Playboy Beauty Works to Save Ill, Dying Children," *Denver Post*, Aug. 4, 1999.

[3] De Cordoba, "Why Susie Krabacher Sold the Sushi Bar."

[4] Ditmer, "Aspen's Angel."

[5] Valerie Richardson, "Helping Ill Haitians Worth It for Centerfold Turned Savior," *Washington Times*, Nov. 28, 2000. Excerpted from a version originally published in *Philanthropy*.

[6] De Cordoba, "Why Susie Krabacher Sold the Sushi Bar."

[7] John Baldoni, *Personal Leadership, Taking Control of Your Work Life* (Rochester Hills, Mich.: Elsewhere Press, 2001), pp. 5–6.

[8] David C. McClelland and David H. Burnham, "Power Is the Great Motivator," *Harvard Business Review*, January 2003, pp. 117–126. Originally published 1976.

[9] David H. Hackworth and Eilhys England, *Steel My Soldiers' Hearts* (New York: Rugged Land, 2002), p. 55.

[10] Ibid., p. 49.

[11] Ibid., pp. 13–62.

[12] Ibid., p. 55.

[13] Ibid., p. 40.

[14] Author interview with David Hackworth, May 20, 2004.

[15] Hackworth and England, *Steel My Soldiers' Hearts*, p. 56.

[16] Ibid., p. 57.

[17] Ibid., p. 56.

[18] Ibid., p. 65.

[19] Ibid., p. 46.

[20] Ibid., p. 69.

[21] Ibid., pp. 69–70.

[22] Ibid., p. 94.

[23] Author interview with David Hackworth.

[24] Hackworth and England, *Steel My Soldiers' Hearts*, p. 58.

[25] Ibid., p. 54.

[26] Author interview with David Hackworth.

[27] Ibid.

[28] Ibid.

[29] Ibid.

[30] Hackworth and England, *Steel My Soldiers' Hearts*, pp. 420–421.

[31] David H. Hackworth and Julie Sherman, *About Face* (New York: Simon & Schuster/Touchstone, 1989), pp. 771–810.

[32] Ibid., pp. 750–51; 804.

[33] Ibid., pp. 811–834.

[34] Author interview with David Hackworth.

## CHAPTER 3

[1] Steve Kroft, "Veronica Guerin," *60 Minutes Classic*, June 16, 1999.

[2] IPI Press Freedom Heroes, "Veronica Guerin," available at www.freemedia.at/IRIReport2.00/20Guerin.htm.

[3] Margaret Morrison, "Who Would Want Veronica Guerin's Job?" *Sunday on Scotland*, Mar. 19, 2000.

[4] Kroft, "Veronica Guerin."

[5] IPI Press Freedom Heroes, "Veronica Guerin."

[6] Morrison, "Who Would Want Veronica Guerin's Job?"

[7] Vincent Canby, "Road to Ubiquity," *New York Times*, July 29, 2003; "Bob Hope," *The Economist*, Aug. 2, 2003; Todd Purdum,

"Bob Hope, Before He Became the Comedy Establishment," *New York Times,* Apr. 20, 2003.

[8] "Satisfaction and Recognition—How Now?" *Potentials* (online newsletter), May 28, 2003.

[9] Fredrick Hertzberg, "One More Time: How Do You Motivate Employees?" *Harvard Business Review*, January 2003, pp. 87–96. Originally published 1968.

[10] Frances Hesselbein, *Hesselbein on Leadership*, foreword by Jim Collins (San Francisco: Jossey-Bass, 2002), pp. xi–xviii.

[11] Author interview with Frances Hesselbein, May 26, 2004.

[12] Ibid.

[13] Ibid.

[14] Ibid.

[15] Ibid.

[16] Ibid.

[17] Ibid.

[18] Hesselbein, *Hesselbein on Leadership*, p. xiv.

[19] Ibid., pp. xiv–xv.

[20] Author interview with Frances Hesselbein.

[21] Hesselbein, *Hesselbein on Leadership*, pp. 55–57.

[22] Ibid., p. 69.

[23] Ibid., pp. 7–11.

[24] Carl Levesque, "A Matter of Being," *Association Management*, Jan. 1, 2003.

[25] Ibid.

[26] Author interview with Frances Hesselbein.

[27] Hesselbein, *Hesselbein on Leadership*, pp. 19–23.

[28] Ibid., pp. 35–36.

[29] Frances Hesselbein, "The Art of Listening," *Leader to Leader* 29 (Summer 2003), pp. 4–6.

[30] Author interview with Frances Hesselbein.

[31] Hesselbein, *Hesselbein on Leadership*, pp. xi–xii.

[32] Levesque, "A Matter of Being."

[33] Ibid.

[34] Ibid.

[35] Author interview with Frances Hesselbein.

[36] Hesselbein, *Hesselbein on Leadership*, pp. 139–142.

[37] Author interview with Frances Hesselbein.

[38] Hesselbein, *Hesselbein on Leadership*, pp. 85–91.

[39] Levesque, "A Matter of Being."

[40] Thich Nhat Hanh, *Anger* (New York: Berkley Books/Riverhead Books, 2001).

[41] Sandi Dolbee, "Just Now: Visiting Buddhist Monk Thich Nhat Hanh Says the Mindful Can Find Heaven on Earth," *San Diego Union-Tribune*, Jan. 29, 2004.

[42] Thich Nhat Hanh, *Creating True Peace* (New York: Free Press, 2003), p. 94.

[43] Ibid., p. 96.

[44] Ibid., pp. 96–101.

[45] Ibid., pp. 107–108.

[46] Thich Nhat Hanh, *Anger*, p. 128.

[47] Thich Nhat Hanh, *Creating True Peace*, p. 85.

[48] Dolbee, "Just Now."

[49] Thich Nhat Hanh, *Anger*, p. 95.

[50] Thich Nhat Hanh, *Creating True Peace*, p. 95.

[51] Heidi Schlumpf, "What Would Buddha Do?" *U.S. Catholic* (Chicago), December 2003.

[52] Ibid.

[53] Thich Nhat Hanh, *Anger*, p. 201.

[54] Ibid., p. 101.

[55] Ibid., p. 195.

[56] Dolbee, "Just Now."

[57] Thich Nhat Hanh, *Creating True Peace*, pp. 29–30.

[58] Ibid., pp. 64–65, 168–169.

[59] Ibid., pp. 189–190.

[60] Schlumpf, "What Would Buddha Do?"

## CHAPTER 4

[1] "Jim Plunkett," *Sports Century*, ESPN Classic, aired originally Dec. 5, 2003; Bob Carter, "Plunkett Kept Coming Back," *Sports Century Biography*, ESPN.com, December 2003.

[2] Patricia Sellers, "P&G: Teaching an Old Dog New Tricks," *Fortune*, May 31, 2004.

[3] Stuart Cranier, *The Ultimate Business Library*, foreword and commentary by Gary Hamel (London: Capstone Publishing, 1997), pp. 54–56.

[4] Ibid., p. 53.

[5] Anya von Bremzen, "25 of the World's Best Food Markets," *Food & Wine*, April 2004.

[6] Bo Burlingham, "The Coolest Small Company in America," *Inc.*, January 2003.

[7] Exceptions to the "poor people's food" offerings are fine chocolates and varietal balsamic vinegars.

[8] Zingerman's Mission Statement, Guiding Principle No. 5 (Ann Arbor, Mich.: Zingerman's Training Inc., 2004).

[9] Zingerman's Mission Statement, Guiding Principles No. 6 and 7 (Ann Arbor, Mich.: Zingerman's Training Inc., 2004).

[10] Author interview with Paul Saginaw, May 24, 2004.

[11] Ibid.

[12] Ibid.

[13] Ari Weinzweig, "3 Steps to Great Finance," Zingerman's review draft, May 26, 2004.

[14] Ibid.

[15] Ibid.

[16] Author interview with Ari Weinzweig, May 24, 2004.

[17] Author interview with Paul Saginaw.

[18] Ibid.

[19] Ibid.

[20] Ibid.

[21] Author interview with Ari Weinzweig, May 26, 2004.

[22] Ari Weinzweig, "Zingerman's 2009: A Food Odyssey" (Ann Arbor, Mich.: Zingerman's Training Inc., 2004).

[23] Author interview with Paul Saginaw.

[24] Weinzweig, "Zingerman's 2009."

## CHAPTER 5

[1] Teresa Carpenter, "John Lewis," in Caroline Kennedy (ed.), *Profiles in Courage for Our Time* (New York: Hyperion, 2002). Ms. Carpenter drew her account from contemporaneous newspaper accounts of Mr. Lewis as well as from his autobiography, *Walking with the Wind: A Memoir of the Movement* with Michael D'Orso.

[2] Adam Clymer, "Daniel Patrick Moynihan, Former Senator from New York, Dies at 76," *New York Times*, Mar. 27, 2003; "Obituary: Daniel Patrick Moynihan," *The Economist*, Mar. 29, 2003.

[3] Comments by Larry Bossidy were made at the *Fortune* Executive Panel at Living Leadership 2003 conference in Atlanta, Ga., on Nov. 5, 2003.

[4] Douglas McGregor *The Human Side of Enterprise* (New York: McGraw-Hill, 1960), quoted in Stuart Cranier, *The Ultimate Business Library*, foreword and commentary by Gary Hamel (London: Capstone Publishing, 1997), pp. 155–158.

[5] Ibid.

[6] Sam Walton with John Huey, *Made in America* (New York: Doubleday/Bantam, 1993), pp. 57–58.

[7] Robert Slater, *The Wal-Mart Decade* (New York: Penguin/Portfolio, 2003), pp. 23–42; Walton, *Made in America*, pp. 1–85.

[8] Walton, *Made in America*, p. 103.

[9] Richard S. Tedlow, *Giants of Enterprise* (New York: Harper Business, 2003), p. 347.

[10] Slater, *Wal-Mart Decade*, pp. 27–32; Walton, *Made in America*, pp. 62–64.

[11] Tedlow, *Giants of Enterprise*, p. 341.

[12] Ibid., pp. 356–359.

[13] Walton, *Made in America*, pp. 161–162.

[14] Ibid., p. 165.

[15] Ibid., pp. 178, 289.

[16] Ibid., p. 180.

[17] Ibid., pp. 180–182.

[18] Ibid., pp. 174–176.

[19] "How Big Can It Grow?" *The Economist*, Apr. 17, 2004.

[20] Walton, *Made in America*, pp. 314–317.

[21] Ibid., pp. 207–217.

[22] Slater, *Wal-Mart Decade*, pp. 71–83.

[23] Earvin "Magic" Johnson with William Novak, *My Life* (New York: Ballantine Books/Fawcett Crest, 1992), pp. 108–109.

[24] Ibid., p. 292.

[25] Ibid., pp. 4–11.

[26] Ibid., pp. 19–20.

[27] Ibid., p. 11.

[28] Ibid., pp. 26–30.

[29] Ibid., pp. 9, 30–31.

[30] Mark Stewart, "Remembering Michigan State–Indiana State Classic 25 Years Later," *Knight-Ridder Tribune News Service (Milwaukee Journal Sentinel)*, Apr. 2, 2004.

[31] Johnson, *My Life*, pp. 222–232.

[32] Ibid., p. 232.

[33] Matthew Kredell, "When Cheers Became Tears; Magic's HIV-Forced Retirement from NBA Affected the Entire World," *Los Angeles Daily News*, Nov. 7, 2001.

[34] Ibid.

[35] "Magic Johnson," *Jet*, Jan. 7, 2002.

[36] Steve Campbell, "Ever the Victor: Diagnosed with HIV 11 Years Ago, Magic Johnson Has Defeated Death—Just as He Said He Would—and Is Smiling All the Way to the Basketball Hall of Fame," *Albany (N.Y.) Times Union*, Sept. 27, 2002.

[37] Web site for Magic Johnson Foundation (Mission Page), www.magicjohnson.org.

[38] Johnson, *My Life*, p. 345.

[39] Ibid., pp. 342–346.

[40] "Magic Johnson," *Jet*.

[41] Campbell, "Ever the Victor."

## CHAPTER 6

[1] Monica Langley, "In Tough Times for CEOs, They Head to Warren Buffett's Table," *Wall Street Journal*, Nov. 14, 2003.

[2] Katharine Graham, *Personal History* (New York: Random House, 1997), pp. 513–515; 524–525; 530–537.

[3] Langley, "Warren Buffett's Table."

[4] James Waldroop and Timothy Butler, *The 12 Bad Habits That Hold Good People Back* (New York: Currency/Doubleday, 2000), p. 164.

[5] Marcus Buckingham and Curt Coffman, *First, Break All the Rules* (New York: Simon & Schuster, 1999).

[6] Daniel Goleman, "What Makes a Leader?" *Harvard Business Review*, November–December 1998, pp. 93–102.

[7] Pat Summitt with Sally Jenkins, *Reach for the Summit* (New York: Broadway Books, 1998), p. 9.

[8] Ibid., p. 21.

[9] Ibid., p.113.

[10] Ibid., p. 30.

[11] Ibid., pp. 11–27.

[12] Ibid., pp. 68–69.

[13] Ibid., pp. 73, 78.

[14] Ibid., pp. 145–152.

[15] Ibid., pp. 60–61; 163–164; 257–261.

[16] Ibid., p. 75.

[17] Ibid., p. 177.

[18] Ibid., pp. 97, 165.

[19] Ibid., pp. 35–36.

[20] Ibid., p. 99.

[21] Ibid., p. 208.

[22] Pat Summitt with Sally Jenkins, *Raise the Roof* (New York: Broadway Books, 1998), pp. 282, 290–291.

[23] Summitt, *Reach for the Summit*, p. 152.

[24] Ibid., pp. 179–181.

[25] Ibid., p. 193.

[26] Ibid., p. 159.

[27] Ibid., pp. 31–32.


## CHAPTER 7

[1] Daniel Lewis, "Fred Rogers, Host of 'Mister Rogers' Neighborhood,' Dies at 74," *New York Times*, Feb. 28, 2003; Davy Rothbart, "A Friend in the Neighborhood," *New York Times*, Feb. 28, 2003; Fred Rogers, "How Do We Make Goodness Attractive?" Acceptance Speech to the Television Hall of Fame, Feb. 27, 1999.

[2] Linda Kulman, "Betty Ford: A First Lady Who Always Takes It Like It Is," *U.S. News & World Report*, Aug. 20–27, 2001.

[3] Ibid.

[4] Renee Montagne, "Interview: Gerald and Betty Ford Discuss Mrs. Ford's Own Battle with Alcohol and How That Struggle Led Her to Help Others at the Betty Ford Clinic," *Morning Edition*, NPR, Oct. 18, 2002.

[5] Kulman, "Betty Ford."

[6] Ibid.

[7] Montagne, "Interview: Gerald and Betty Ford."

[8] Bob Nelson, "The Ironies of Motivation" *Strategy & Leadership*, January/February 1999.

[9] Ibid.

[10] Marcus Buckingham and Curt Coffman, *First, Break All the Rules* (New York: Simon & Schuster, 1999), pp. 153-63.

[11] Marlo Thomas and friends, *The Right Words at the Right Time* (New York: Atria Books, 2002), pp. 276–277.

[12] Ibid., pp. 213–216.

[13] Judith R. Gordon, *Organizational Behavior: A Diagnostic Approach*, 5th ed. (Upper Saddle River, N.J.: Prentice-Hall, 1996), pp. 134–135.

[14] Mary Kay Ash, *Miracles Happen* (New York: Quill, 2003), p. 160.

[15] Ibid., p. 174.

[16] Ibid., pp. 1–10.

[17] Ibid., p. 17.

[18] Ibid., pp. 22, 26.

[19] Ibid., pp. 22–33.

[20] Ibid., pp. 20–21, 103.

[21] Ibid., p. 147.

[22] Ibid., pp. 150–159.

[23] Ibid., pp. 150–159; Jim Underwood, *More than a Pink Cadillac* (New York: McGraw-Hill, 2003), pp. 18, 79, 95–100.

[24] Ash, *Miracles Happen*, pp. 168–171.

[25] Ibid., pp. 1–52.

[26] Ibid., pp. 43–52.

[27] Ibid., pp. 55–57, 75–81.

[28] Ibid., p. 164.

[29] Ibid., pp. 60–61; Underwood, *More than a Pink Cadillac*, pp. 14, 22.

[30] Underwood, *More than a Pink Cadillac*, pp. 18, 23, 41–42, 79, 95–100.

[31] Ash, *Miracles Happen*, p. 181.

[32] Ibid., pp. 179–180.

[33] Ibid., p. 179.

[34] Ibid., p. 179.

## CHAPTER 8

[1] Greg Myre, "A Healer of Terror Victims Becomes One," *New York Times*, Sept. 11, 2003.

[2] "Sergio Vieira de Mello" (obituary), *The Economist*, Aug. 23, 2003; Paul Lewis, "A Diplomat's Life: Sergio de Vieira de Mello, 55, of the U.N., Dies: A Shining Reputation Built on Tough Tasks," *New York Times*, Aug. 20, 2003; Steven Erlanger, "'I Should Always Believe in Journalists,' He Said, Adding 'Please Pray for Me,'" *New York Times*, Aug. 24, 2003.

[3] Malcolm Brown, *The Imperial War Museum Book of the Somme* (London: Pan Books 1997), pp. 336–337.

[4] Robert Dallek, *Kennedy: An Unfinished Life* (New York: Simon & Schuster, 2003), pp. 90–96.

[5] Douglas Brinkley, "Tour of Duty: John Kerry in Vietnam," *The Atlantic Monthly*, December 2003, pp. 47–60 (excerpted from Douglas Brinkley, *Tour of Duty: John Kerry and the Vietnam War* [New York: William Morrow, 2004]).

[6] Larry McMurtry, *Crazy Horse* (New York: Penguin Lives, 1999), pp. 111–113.

[7] Ibid., pp. 1–13; Stephen E. Ambrose, *Crazy Horse and Custer: The Parallel Lives of Two American Warriors* (New York: Random House/Anchor Books, 1996).

[8] McMurtry, *Crazy Horse*, pp. 1–13; Ambrose, *Crazy Horse and Custer*, pp. 37–57.

[9] McMurtry, *Crazy Horse*, pp. 33–36; Ambrose, *Crazy Horse and Custer*, pp. 67–69.

[10] Ambrose, *Crazy Horse and Custer*, pp. 135–137.

[11] McMurtry, *Crazy Horse*, pp. 89–96; Ambrose, *Crazy Horse and Custer*, pp. 411–417.

[12] McMurtry, *Crazy Horse*, pp. 101–102.

[13] Ibid., pp. 100–105; Ambrose, *Crazy Horse and Custer*, pp. 437–438.

[14] McMurtry, *Crazy Horse*, pp. 106–110; Ambrose, *Crazy Horse and Custer*, pp. 451–457.

[15] McMurtry, *Crazy Horse*, pp. 69–71; Ambrose, *Crazy Horse and Custer*, pp. 338–342.

[16] Ambrose, *Crazy Horse and Custer*, p. 457.

[17] Ibid., pp. 461–463.

[18] Ibid., pp. 463–473.

[19] McMurtry, *Crazy Horse*, pp. 147–148.

[20] Ibid., pp. 1–3. McMurtry attributes the quote about Indians smiling when they see the monument to Ian Frazier, *Great Plains* (New York: Farrar, Straus & Giroux, 1989).

## CHAPTER 9

[1] David Gergen, *Eyewitness to Power: The Essence of Leadership Nixon to Clinton* (New York: Simon & Schuster, 2000), p. 203.

[2] Chris Matthews, "Interview with Christopher Cox," Hardball MSNBC, CA-Rep 6.07.04.

[3] Taylor Branch, *Parting the Waters: America in the King Years, 1954–63* (New York: Simon & Schuster, 1988), pp. 124–125, 129–135.

[4] Linda Kulman with David Enrich, "Rosa Parks: She Sat Down and the World Turned Around," *U.S. News & World Report*, Aug. 20–27, 2001.

[5] Ibid.

[6] Ibid.

[7] Ibid.

[8] Ibid.

[9] Christine MacDonald, "Rosa Parks Scholarships Impart Pride," *Detroit News*, Mar. 2, 2004.

[10] *Webster's New World Dictionary*, Third College Edition (Cleveland & New York: Webster's New World, 1988).

[11] Sun Tzu, *The Art of War: The Denma Translation* (Boston & London: Shambhala, 2002), p. 3.

[12] Curtis Schleier, "Intel Co-founder Robert Noyce: He Invented His Way to the Top," *Investor's Business Daily*, Nov. 5, 2001. From *Business Leaders & Success* (New York: McGraw-Hill, 2004), pp. 223–224.

[13] William Shakespeare, *Henry V*, Act 4, Scene 3, lines 60–67.

[14] Stuart Cranier, *The Ultimate Business Library*, foreword and commentary by Gary Hamel (London: Capstone Publishing, 1997), pp. 95–97.

[15] Margot Morrell and Stephanie Capparell, *Shackleton's Way: Leadership Lessons from the Great Antarctic Explorer*, preface by Alexandra Shackleton (New York: Viking, 2001). The photograph of the expedition's crew playing soccer appears on the cover of this book.

[16] Ernest Shackleton, *South: The Endurance Expedition*, introduction by Fergus Fleming (1919; reprint, New York: Penguin Classics 2002), pp. xx–xxiii.

[17] Actor/director Kenneth Branagh conveyed the explorer as a dynamic and passionate fundraiser in his the drama about the expedition, *Shackleton; The Greatest Adventure Story of All Time* (A&E Home Video).

[18] F. A. Worsley, *Endurance*, preface by Patrick O'Brian (1931; reprint, New York & London: W.W. Norton 2000), pp. 267–268.

[19] Ibid., pp. 30–33; Shackleton, *South*, pp. xxv–xxvi.

[20] Worsley, *Endurance*, p. 12.

[21] Shackleton, *South*, pp. 80–81; Worsley, *Endurance*, pp. 13, 29, 53.

[22] Worsley, *Endurance*, pp. 53, 62.

[23] Ibid., p. 181.

[24] Ibid., pp. 105–106; Shackleton, *South*, p. 107.

[25] Shackleton, *South*, pp. 201–204.

[26] Ibid., p. 214.

[27] Worsley, *Endurance*, p. 295.

[28] Ibid., p. 298.

[29] Ibid., p. 53.

## MOTIVATION HANDBOOK

[1] The author would like to acknowledge that ideas expressed in this handbook section were explored in a previous work, John Baldoni and Eric Harvey, *180 Ways to Walk the Motivation Talk* (Dallas, Tex.: Walk the Talk Company, 2002)

[2] Patricia Sellers, "P&G: How to Teach an Old Dog New Tricks," *Fortune*, May 31, 2004.

[3] John Baldoni, *Personal Leadership, Taking Control of Your Work Life* (Rochester, Mich.: Elsewhere Press, 2001), pp. 3–11.

[4] Linda Tischler, "60 Seconds with George Foreman," *Fast Company*, June 2004.

## CITATIONS FOR CHAPTER OPENING QUOTES

### CHAPTER 1

Bill Choyke, "Southwest Flies Its Own Route," *The Virginian-Pilot & The Ledger-Star*, Sept. 15, 2003.

### CHAPTER 2

David H. Hackworth and Eilhys England, *Steel My Soldiers' Hearts* (New York: Rugged Land, 2002), p. 71.

### CHAPTER 3

Bob Nelson, "The Ironies of Motivation," *Strategy & Business*, January/February 1999.

Thich Nhat Hanh, *Creating True Peace* (New York: Free Press, 2003), p. 93.


## CHAPTER 4
Zingerman's Mission Statement, Guiding Principles No. 6 and 7 (Ann Arbor, Mich.: Zingerman's Training Inc., 2004).


## CHAPTER 5
Sam Walton with John Huey, *Made in America* (New York: Doubleday/Bantam, 1993), pp. 57–58.

Earvin "Magic" Johnson with William Novak, *My Life* (New York: Ballantine Books/Fawcett Crest, 1992), p. 359.


## CHAPTER 6
Pat Summitt with Sally Jenkins, *Reach for the Summit* (New York: Broadway Books, 1998), p. 37.


## CHAPTER 7
Mary Kay Ash, *Pearls of Wisdom*, quoted in Mary Kay Ash, *Miracles Happen* (New York: Quill, 2003), p. 177.


## CHAPTER 8
Stephen E. Ambrose, *Crazy Horse and Custer: The Parallel Lives of Two American Warriors* (New York: Random House/Anchor Books, 1996), pp. 465–466. (This quote is attributed to Crazy Horse by Major V. T. McGillicuddy, who befriended him.)


## CHAPTER 9
F. A. Worsley, *Endurance*, preface by Patrick O'Brian (1931; reprint, New York & London: W.W. Norton, 2000), p. 84.

# Index

## About the Author

**John Baldoni** is a leadership communications consultant who works with Fortune 500 companies such as Ford Motor Company, Kellogg's, and Pfizer, as well as with nonprofits including the University of Michigan. He also speaks on leadership topics to audiences in the public and private sectors. His articles are widely published and have appeared in such publications as the *Harvard Management Communications Letter, Leader to Leader,* and the *Wharton Leadership Digest.* John is the author of five books on leadership, including *Great Communication Secrets of Great Leaders.* Readers are welcome to visit his leadership resource Web site at www.johnbaldoni.com.